THE DELUSION

How faith in the NHS is impacting our health

MICHAEL
CHRISTOPHER

CRANTHORPE
— MILLNER —
PUBLISHERS

Copyright © Michael Christopher (2025)

The right of Michael Christopher to be identified as author of this work has been asserted by them in accordance with section 77 and 78 of the Copyright, Designs and Patents Act 1988.

All rights reserved. No part of this publication may be reproduced, stored in a retrieval system, or transmitted in any form or by any means, electronic, mechanical, photocopying, recording, or otherwise, without the prior permission of the publishers.

Any person who commits any unauthorised act in relation to this publication may be liable to criminal prosecution and civil claims for damages.

First published by Cranthorpe Millner Publishers (2025)

ISBN 978-1-80378-289-8 (Paperback)

www.cranthorpemillner.com

Cranthorpe Millner Publishers

CONTENTS

PREFACE	i
INTRODUCTION	1
PART ONE: THE NHS	21
1. PROPAGANDA	23
Trying to split the Reds	
2. CLAPPED OUT?	46
Tales from COVID	
3. GENESIS	70
The Creation Myth	
4. GUILTY PARTIES	81
How politicians have weaponised the NHS	
5. STATE OF AFFAIRS	98
Philosophy and ideology	
6. PRIMARY COLOURS	117
General Practice	
7. OUT OF SIGHT...	138
Mental Health	
PART TWO: THE REST	151
8. SINGAPORE	153
The city in a garden	
9. AUSTRALIA	172
Splendid Isolation	

10. ACROSS THE CHANNEL *The Champions' League*	188
11. ALL AROUND THE WORLD *Different strokes for different folks*	194
12. LIES, DAMN LIES AND... *Statistics*	204
13. A TALE OF TWO BABIES *Singapore vs London*	219
CONCLUSION	237
AUTHOR'S NOTE	249
REFERENCES	253

PREFACE

Westminster Abbey, London, July 5th, 2023

The candles are lit. The cathedral is ready. The great and the good – the prime minister, leaders of the main political parties and senior members of the royal family – file silently into the pews. Expensive polished shoes tap on ancient flagstones. The gentle undulating hum of organ music is heard in the background. The atmosphere is reverential, but not sorrowful. Solemn, rather than funereal. Westminster Abbey, the national pulpit that has seen almost a millennium of monarchs crowned, is the setting for a celebration.

This is the building that contains the tombs of Edward I, Elizabeth I and her cousin, Mary, Queen of Scots; the final resting place of Charles Dickens, Sir Isaac Newton, and the bones of over three thousand other souls that have, in different ways, contributed to our island story.

Today, the nation has come together to give thanks, under God, though this is not primarily a religious ceremony, but a political occasion. For today, we have come to give thanks for the National Health Service (NHS) on its seventy-fifth anniversary. The service is led by the Dean of Westminster, the Very Reverend Dr David Hoyle. He does not hold back in his bidding:

'We gather in thanksgiving for both the grace of God and the grace and glory that is the NHS. We celebrate seventy-five years of public witness to the common good. Born of the radical conviction that we must care for one another, the National Health Service sets before us all the better angels of our nature. Here is high principle translated into best practice. Here is the steady dedication of those who, for us, face pain and fear, know life and death, tragedy and near miracle, and return another day to do that again. Here is a courage tested to its limits. Here is a virtuoso capacity for innovation; a dedicated and lively expertise. Here is love made manifest.'[1]

So, what is wrong with that, you may ask?

Well, nothing. But if the NHS really is *that* great, why is its performance so mediocre? If it is 'love made manifest', then the rest of the world should surely have already replaced their own healthcare systems with our NHS model?

There is, of course, nothing radical about the conviction that we must care for one another; plenty of other countries manage that without our NHS, or indeed any NHS of their own. The NHS is indeed radical, as you might expect of a service 'founded' by a radical socialist. By hijacking Christian language and concepts of morality, and perpetuating the unsaid belief that without the NHS there would be no healthcare – or caring for each other – *at all*, the proponents of state-run healthcare construct a shield against all criticism that none can penetrate.

Dictators of totalitarian states would kill for this sort of publicity. One can almost imagine, in a hidden location on the outskirts of Pyongyang, Kim Jong-Un watching the subtitled proceedings with interest, while dipping an observant pen into an inkwell as he starts making notes.

There may be clowns to the left and jokers to the right, but politically, the UK is stuck in the middle. We are not a country given to extremes and the British have never been a profoundly ideological people. Despite Karl Marx having written the Communist Manifesto in London, and not withstanding all those student posters of Che Guevara, communism never took hold, nor has any far-left government been formed. Whenever a leftist Labour leader such as Corbyn gets within a whiff of power, they usually have the door slammed on them with immense force. On the other side of the equation, post-war at least, there has never been anything other than the faintest of political murmurings from the far-right, unlike most other large countries in Europe. Demagoguery and nationalism seem to fall flat in this nation of gardens, stamp collectors and shopkeepers. Thatcherism, though successful at the ballot box, was never an ideology shared by most of the British public, let alone the Conservative party itself, where Thatcherites were always a minority.

So, no cigar chomping pinstripe loadsamoney, nor any olive-clothed hair-shirted commie, can gain much traction. But while we may not have a Lenin, or a Hitler (or even a Trump), *boy* do we have a Bevan. Nye Bevan has a legacy most elected politicians can only dream of.

Why?

Because Bevan was the 'founder' of the UK's National Health Service (NHS), in 1948: the original high priest of this deified service. If the NHS is Mormonism, he is Joseph Smith with the plates of gold.

The worship of this NHS, despite overwhelming evidence that other alternative systems abroad not only exist, but are better, is an oddity in the national psyche. Conservatives, Labour, and the Liberals come and go in general elections. Market forces and social democratic planning trend up and down in fashion. Outside the NHS, politics is all centre-ground, with never more than a little tinkering around a moderate centre-left, centre-right fulcrum. But inside the NHS, socialism reigns, and is left untouched – an outlier sticking out as an ideological sore thumb.

In order to examine the deep reverence the British people have for this service, where this devotion comes from, and the politics, philosophy and economics behind it, we must first explore the mistaken belief that the NHS is, through its morals, or its delivery, somehow the best healthcare system in the world. To do this successfully, it is essential to avoid any ideological preconceptions. We must start with a completely blank sheet of paper.

It is my view that ideology and healthcare do not mix well, and that any ideological approach can only be justified by resorting to empiricism: what 'works the best' by producing the best outcome for the greatest number of people. No system is perfect, but a utilitarian standpoint is a good start and will lead to an open mind. This book aims to provide a critique from the centre of political ground, which puts us firmly in the realm of mixed, multi-payer systems that outperform the NHS, such as those in most of Western Europe and Australia. Our healthcare options are not limited to the black and white NHS vs 'American model' thinking portrayed in the media. In fact, there is a huge English-speaking country, the size of a continent, that has stumbled upon as near-perfect a model of healthcare as is possible in the twenty-first century. And it is not the United States of America. I have been fortunate to work in several healthcare systems in three different countries, and have met and treated expatriates from all over Europe and North America, hearing the opinions they have of their own countries' healthcare systems and the way they perceive the NHS.

To clarify, any criticisms of the NHS discussed in this book are very much of the institution, its structural weaknesses, and failures, rather than of the staff who work in it. We have some of the best frontline medical staff in the world and we certainly have the best GPs, but having paid a fortune for their training, we overload them with rushed appointments, make their lives a complete misery and then stand by helplessly as they vanish off abroad.

My personal experience is mostly as a general practitioner, so I will be speaking from atop the soapbox of primary care, but the overall message and examination of other systems applies equally to secondary care, as we will see.

I have tried to avoid using anecdotes, certainly when directly involving patients. This is not a 'confessions of a GP' book, and I have tried to concentrate on the bigger picture. Either you (or a relative) may have had good care on the NHS, under diligent doctors and caring nurses. You may feel you have had good treatment and get slightly angry or defensive amid any criticisms of the service. But we must try to put emotions to one side and think objectively. Was your care good thanks to the NHS, or were you lucky enough to have good doctors and good nurses who worked hard to treat you *despite* the NHS?

Some patients have excellent experiences of the frontline NHS and some have heartbreaking disasters. We must resort to a dispassionate look at what works and what does not, to get any sort of handle on reality. Otherwise, we end up with 'my anecdote is better than your anecdote' – an intractable argument of the Oxford vs Cambridge, Lennon vs McCartney, Liverpool vs Manchester United type. Nobody wins (though my choice is Oxford, Lennon, and Liverpool, but if you find yourself in instant disagreement, you rather prove the point).

It may not seem like it, but almost all the care you receive in the NHS, could, by unseen forces, have been made slightly worse *by* the NHS. Your care could have been a bit better had there been no understaffing, for example. The wait for your scan could have been a little less if there were more scanners; if resources were allocated according to need and not by central government planning.

For every anecdote of good care there are anecdotes of bad care; patients waiting hours for an ambulance or on hospital trolleys. There are patients suffering unnecessary pain or delayed cancer diagnoses, or mental health patients falling through the cracks in the system.

Trying to compare is impossible, and the purpose of this book is not to prove that the NHS is bad, or good. It is to highlight the delusion that the NHS is the *only*, or *best*, option. Speaking to a wide variety of expatriates over the course of my career made me realise that the NHS is not, as many of us have been made to believe, the envy of the world.

During the COVID pandemic, the NHS escaped serious criticism, despite the death toll, and politicians took the flak. Our elected officials may deserve some blame, but responsibility for the poor performance also lies with the NHS and Public Health model. Not with the doctors and nurses, who adapted brilliantly, but with the lumbering monolithic approach to procurement, weak planning and basic incompetence at the top that has dogged the NHS for years.

Unfortunately, it is impossible to imagine an open debate regarding how the NHS could be reformed, updated, or even replaced, without images of a book-of-revelation style apocalypse being forced on the nation; of patients being bodily removed from their hospital beds and 'thrown onto the streets' – a recurring phrase for NHS fundamentalists. However, there are changes that could be implemented on a smaller scale, and the message of this book is to try and think logically, not ideologically, about our roles as doctors and patients, and to open our minds to the possibility of creating the sort of healthcare system we deserve.

INTRODUCTION

The NHS and healthcare are huge topics, so huge in fact that it is important to define the premise of this book, otherwise we risk going down a series of rabbit holes. Like the white rabbit of *Alice in Wonderland* we are of course running out of time, or rather, the NHS is.

In the first half of the book, I focus on the NHS experience, including the COVID-19 pandemic and how the politicised nature of government-run healthcare enabled politicians to destroy any effective response to the crisis, resulting in delays to diagnosis and treatment for non-covid conditions for years to come. I discuss the politics of the NHS, and how it has become weaponised in public debate, including a detailed look at the ideology and dogmatic philosophy that underpins it. I also describe life 'at the coalface' in primary care, and some of the dysfunction in the system, before highlighting mental health as an area of concern.

The second half of the book explores how healthcare works in other countries and suggests alternative models we could examine, starting with Singapore and Australia, where I have first-hand experience, before looking at both US and European models, which utilise a mixture of state and private insurance.

Being assaulted with endless statistics would bore the pants off most readers, as it certainly would me, so I have tried to roll the statistics into a shapely ball and put them all in one chapter, using examples that will hopefully be relevant and thought provoking, rather than delivering an overly detailed examination of healthcare systems and state insurance models around the world, which I have no doubt would be an extremely dry subject.

Finally, I have included a chapter exploring my own experience on the other side of the curtain, as the relative of a patient, which led to a direct comparison of the UK and Singaporean systems.

Before we begin, though, let us consider the title of the book – *The NHS Delusion*. The title was chosen as a deliberate homage to Richard Dawkins' book *The God Delusion*, an apt analogy, for the NHS has been repeatedly described as 'the nearest thing we in Britain have to a national religion'. This is rather an odd quote; unlike many Western European countries, we *do* have a national religion, and an established church, though there are far more people breaking bread and drinking wine at the altar of the NHS than there are elderly worshippers warming the pews in the dwindling congregations of the Church of England.

Let us take the Oxford definition of a delusion, and try to define what we mean by *The NHS Delusion*. A delusion is considered to be: '*a false belief or judgment about external reality, held despite incontrovertible evidence to the contrary, occurring especially in mental conditions*'.

Assuming that most people in the United Kingdom in the third decade of the twenty-fist century are not suffering from 'mental conditions', we will concentrate on the first two parts of the sentence. Having defined what a delusion is, what delusion are we talking about exactly? In its simplest form, it could be written as:

The NHS is the best healthcare system in the world.

Of course, there are plenty of dissenters to this, at least post-COVID, and it is possible, using a range of statistics, to disprove this sentence, which is what the definition of a delusion requires – in order to be a delusion, it must be demonstrably false.

But, as per religious belief, faith (for this is what we are taking about), must be non-falsifiable, and not amenable to rational argument. The above delusion is eminently falsifiable, so does not quite hit the nail on the head as far as I am concerned.

The delusion may be better put this way:

The NHS is the most moral and civilised healthcare system in the world.

This is more of an article of faith than the first definition and leads us more into the moral and unfalsifiable. However, a more prosaic delusion, and one that I think is shared by most of the public, is as follows:

The NHS would be the best healthcare system in the world, if it was funded properly.

Again, we can use evidence with this one, rather than

deontological ethics. As we will see in later chapters, there is no exact link between money spent and healthcare outcomes. The two foreign countries I have worked in (both former British colonies, incidentally) spend less on healthcare than we do, yet have far better results and patient satisfaction levels than the NHS.

Since the COVID-19 pandemic, NHS spending has gone through the roof, and we now spend roughly as much, if not more, than most equivalent countries: over one hundred and fifty billion pounds a year, in fact, and climbing fast[2]. Yet for all this money, what has been the result?

The NHS is not an underfunded underdog, fighting against the odds to overachieve. It is a hugely funded behemoth that, despite all its potential, fundamentally and massively *underachieves*, rather like the million-to-one-shot *Rocky* movie in reverse.

There are smaller derivate delusions as well, none of which are true, as we will show later in this book. Here are a few of them:

- **The NHS is unique to the UK**
- **The NHS is the only healthcare system free at the point of delivery**
- **The NHS is the envy of the world**
- **The NHS is the only system funded primarily by taxation**
- **Many countries around the world want to copy the NHS model**
- **Healthcare in other developed countries is neither**

free nor equitable

To stay with religion a moment longer, the wishful thinking involved in our perception of the NHS is remarkable. We want, desperately want, it to be the best, or the most moral, or 'almost the best if only it was funded properly' healthcare system in the world. It is a matter of national pride, of nostalgia, of *When We Were Very Young* and *The House at Pooh Corner*. We cherish it, as we cherish the BBC, David Attenborough, Michael Palin and Margo Leadbetter. We love the NHS as an old uncle who was once a brilliant biochemist but has started to collect dandruff in his lapels, thumbprints on his glasses, and is 'at risk of falls'.

However, *wanting* the NHS to be the best does not make it true. Our almost wilful worship of our homegrown behemoth has blinded us to the fact that other countries do healthcare better, not by following the complex mix of public and private insurance as per the demonised US model, but by using systems all of their own.

But, as human beings, we struggle to let delusions go, clinging on to them with ever-whitening knuckles. The myth thus spills out in broadcast and print media; the system may need to be tweaked, or better funded, but ultimately, we do not really want to consider anything else. It is the ultimate 'cling to nurse for fear of something worse' and embodies, rather ironically for a socialist centralised planned healthcare model, a deep lowercase 'c' conservatism within the British public.

For the sake of simplicity, we will stick to the first iteration of the delusion I have spelled out above. This book is not 'The NHS Delusions' after all, so we will keep things singular. The second 'delusion' does bear looking at though. Why do we think that the NHS is the most moral and civilised healthcare system in the world? Because Nye Bevan said so? Because it has been repeated *ad nauseum* by the BBC in particular?

Assumedly, it is because the lofty 'founding principle of the NHS' – that healthcare should be available at the point of clinical need and not based on ability to pay. I could not agree more with this sentiment. I am sure many Europeans and people in different countries around the globe would not tolerate anything less, and therefore also expect healthcare free at the point of delivery, without being based on your American Express status. What is bizarre about this sentiment is that most of the British public truly believe that the UK *is the only country where this happens*. If you believe this then you are, regrettably, in factual error.

Other countries are perfectly able to deliver models of healthcare completely different to the NHS, with better outcomes, more accessibility, quicker treatment, and more public satisfaction, without casting their eyes at the UK and our supposed moral and civilised superiority. This wilful lack of knowledge about the ninety-nine percent of the world's population who do not have access to the NHS is a disaster. Such parochialism stifles reform, blames the wrong people for NHS failures, and worst of all leaves the state (in the form of lamentably weak politicians) in charge of our health. Yes, we have amazing doctors and nurses, and their competence and hard work keep the whole system afloat, just about. But the excellent staff do their jobs well despite the NHS, not because of it.

In discussions of the NHS, truisms always abound, whereas

nuance does not. When considering the ethics of healthcare delivery, asserting the need to be 'moral' and 'civilised' is something of a 'no shit sherlock' moment. What does it mean, anyway, when we say the NHS is the most moral and civilised form of healthcare? It cannot mean 'free at the point of delivery', as other countries also manage this. It cannot be that it is funded by taxation, as many other countries also use taxes to fund healthcare. We have no moral superiority there.

A socialist might say that the moral and civilised aspect of the NHS results from the fact that it is 'owned' and run by the state on behalf of the public. Other countries may have government funded healthcare but they do not also rely on the state to both run the service *and* deliver it, so this is a genuine difference. At the apex of a system funded, managed, and provided by the state, is the government itself. And goodness, you really do need an *awful* lot of faith in your elected officials and civil servants to be comfortable with this state of affairs. You would have to believe that the government of any political stripe (in theory a left-leaning Labour Government, but in reality *any* government) is best left alone to provide your cradle to grave healthcare. You would need to believe that government is both uniquely benevolent, *and* competent to carry these roles out. But our experience of the pandemic must, surely, have disabused us of this notion, ensuring that we are wary of trusting ourselves to the tender mercies of the political wing of the NHS ever again.

Despite almost complete ignorance as to how it works, US healthcare seems to attract opprobrium. It manifests itself as an easy 'go-to' comparison, and thus demonisation. This is encouraged by those with a political agenda, such as the left wing of the Labour Party and a few on the fringes on the US Democratic party, who find a natural home via outlets such as the BBC.

This is odd, as many Americans are happy with their system. Indeed, the majority of Americans enjoy access to the most advanced healthcare technologies in the world, hence the phenomenon of foreign leaders, the rich, and the occasional crowdfunded child travelling there to be treated for supposedly incurable conditions.

There is also an unfailing hatred of the profit motive in healthcare in the UK, an assumption that greed would play an automatic role in a private or mixed system. This seems profoundly ideological and is not healthy, as it ignores many countries with insurance funds that are not-for-profit, such as France and Germany. And even (horror of horrors) the US.

The private sector, not just in healthcare but generally, is demonised in the UK to such an extent that the public seem to have forgotten that private sector taxes fund the welfare state and the NHS, and are the only way the service can continue to grow. This certainly seems to have been the attitude of government ministers during COVID, who shut down the private sector, throttling the NHS of its source of funding and relying on a ruinous mixture of increasing government debt and money-printing to keep the welfare state from collapsing entirely.

This knee jerk belief that the state or government should fund, run, and deliver healthcare creates an uncritical environment wholly detrimental to identifying areas of improvement. When things go wrong, the government, specifically 'the Tories' are blamed for underfunding, even when their plans barely differ from those of Labour. Sometimes even staff themselves are held responsible: usually managers, but also, in a worrying new trend, GPs, and, to a lesser extent, consultants. This blame, at its most extreme, takes the form of abuse of frontline NHS staff, which is ludicrous: those are the very people who keep the whole show on the road. Swearing at a doctor or receptionist because you have been kept waiting, or cannot get an appointment or the medication you need at a certain time, is rather like blaming flight attendants for airline delays or cancellations.

All of this begs the question: why are we not blaming the NHS itself? Even people who should know better, sceptical and critical voices from *Private Eye* to the *Lancet*, will witter on about structural issues and problems, while never blaming the system itself. Instead, these voices perform verbal somersaults and cherry pick statistics to inform their conformation bias. But might it be time to consider the possibility that a few tweaks and more money are not the answer, and that what we actually need is a wholesale reform?

While we will be looking at the NHS in the first part of this book, and later looking at systems in other countries, it is true that the US system is not one that would be a suitable model for the UK. It would be both political unviable and ruinously expensive. There are, also, far better systems in English-speaking countries that offer universal care without bankrupting the economy. However, just because American healthcare would be a poor fit for the UK, it does not follow that we should ape the former Soviet Union. That economic basket case was no model for *anything*, whatever Jeremy Corbyn or his director of communication, Seamus Milne, would have you believe. At present, we are far nearer the Soviet model than the American one, in appearance and attitude as much as anything else.

On a recent visit to my local A&E with a serious but manageable complaint, I noticed puddles on the floor near the entrance; half the building looked like a portacabin that had been welded onto the main hospital; there was exposed and sinister-looking wiring everywhere; cracks and gaps in the walls had been covered with masking tape or what appeared to be bin bags; a strip light flickered aimlessly before spluttering out of life altogether; and there was ripped lining on many of the seats.

To continue the analogy with the Soviet Union: when the Germans invaded in 1941, Hitler famously said that they 'only needed to kick the door in and the whole rotten structure would come crashing down'. This A&E would not even need a kick. A well-aimed fart would probably suffice.

It comes to a pretty pass that recently displaced persons from Ukraine are willing to risk Russian bombs and bullets to get healthcare in their own country, rather than put themselves at the mercy of the NHS[3]. This has a certain ironic flavour, as the concept of the Potemkin village originates from the Crimea. The NHS is, in some ways, the ultimate Potemkin village: an external facade constructed by politicians to give a false impression of the situation that really exists within.

When I worked in A&E, the consultants were hardly ever there, and if they were, they rarely saw patients. I recall one exception at a London hospital, when a venerable consultant turned out up at 4am in his pyjamas, smelling just a teeny bit of 'the fumes of wine'. But that was a different era. These days, given that demand has become stratospheric, A&E is not for the faint hearted or the doddery.

I have been in medical emergency centres in Spain, Australia, Singapore, China, Germany, and the United States. The A&E I recently visited as a patient was the worst, not by a small amount, but by miles. God, it must be embarrassing to work in. Even the wretched vending machine didn't function properly: my Snickers bar got stuck, leaving me both a little poorer and a lot hungrier. I watched a heroic guide dog sitting next his elderly master for over four hours. Even this exemplary canine looked miserable.

Still, it was impossible not to notice the sheer stoicism of the British People, typified by their ability to queue for long periods of time. If any nationality was bred to sit and tolerate long waits in A&E, it is the British. Everyone was calm and tolerant. I sometimes consider the possibility that, were we a little less tolerant, a little less calm and forgiving, public opinion might have turned on the NHS a long time ago.

The dilapidated A&E building led me to recall my NHS University Teaching Hospital. It was similar to the *Ministry of Love*, having small windows and security gates, and being encircled by barbed wire. A constant symbol, if not of a totalitarian super state, then at least of the grim reaper, waving a scythe and egg-timer forebodingly, as if to say, 'your time will come, when I will swallow you up in my dark belly, and you will be as specks of dust carried up and away of the wind out of the chimney of the hospital crematorium'.

The NHS may be many things but, with a few notable exceptions, a builder of beautiful buildings it is not. Our hospital could have been designed by a sadist obsessed with Dante's *Divine Comedy*: 'abandon hope, all ye who enter here'.

In the evenings, three of the hospital's four facades were in complete darkness, the many windows all with their blinds closed. Situated on the north facing side, light streamed out form the Accident and Emergency department where, in the small hours there remained a constant stream of medical admissions, so the lights never went off and the furnaces of hell kept on burning.

A cluster of patients loitered outside the hospital entrance day and night, whatever the weather. There were the smokers, furiously puffing away with their drip stands trailing behind them, and there were always a number of patients on their mobile phones, which used to be banned on hospital grounds. There were also patients who were there for more sinister reasons, who spat their opiate medication into their hankies to be sold for 'street'. And finally, wandering amongst the rest would be a handful of vacant, gormless patients clad in their dressing gowns, staring into space or bleating to themselves, unable to contemplate the horror of it all.

People in this country put up with a lot. And yet, despite it all, the collective belief that the NHS is uniquely special, and that other countries are envious of it, still seems all pervasive. This even as the country gets poorer and its healthcare outcomes fall further and further behind.

There are a couple of analogies that can be seen as relevant to the parochial British attachment to the NHS and its supposed excellence. The first is that of our great national airline, British Airways. After being amalgamated into a single entity in the Seventies, BA began life as a nationalised company. It was privatised in the Eighties and soon went from strength to strength with a large route network, driven by excellent marketing campaigns. Innovations such as the first lie-flat beds in business class made BA an industry leader.

And what has happened since then? BA has rested on its laurels, started cost-cutting, and failed to innovate. All of which has resulted in the company being taken over by airlines in other countries. The BA premium product became outdated, and the company has since become a byword for inefficiency, poor customer service, cut price call centre rudeness, and exorbitant costs.

And yet, despite all of this, many people I know, who rarely travel with BA, persist in the belief that it is the best airline in the world. This in part, perhaps, because they are still so expensive. Meanwhile, those who have no choice but to travel with them frequently see them for what they are: a diminished brand that nonetheless still commands a strange loyalty. One only needs to fly with Qatar Airways or Singapore Airlines, or use their hub airports, to realise we are in third world status when it comes to our airlines and airport infrastructure. This mirrors the British obsession with the NHS and the persistent view that it is the best, or at least would be if it had a bit more money.

Another area in which we appear to be happy to accept utter mediocrity is the management of the English national football team. As many in the UK will know, Gareth Southgate was picked to coach the English national side following a scandal involving his predecessor. This happened because of the paucity of good candidates and the fact he was already working inside the Football Association and could be put forward as a sort of 'next in line'. Yet his managerial credentials were extremely poor. He had never won anything as a manger, and his sole achievement seems to have been getting Middlesbrough FC relegated from the Premier League. In his first three tournaments England benefited from a very favourable draw to reach the latter stages, but as soon as they came up against a half decent side, they lost. Southgate's tactics were noted to be both unimaginative and conservative. Put politely, he was a serial loser. Yet this did not stop a groundswell of approval from the media with their oh-so-premature 'football's coming home' chants, and all this before England had actually *won* anything.

Yet this mediocre manager, whose sole qualifications seem to be his media approachability and 'take the knee' approach to political correctness, was the second highest paid manager in world football at the Qatar 2022 World Cup, raking in almost five million pounds per year[4]. Indeed, he earned only slightly less than the managers of France and Argentina (the two eventual finalists) combined. Yet the belief persists that, though he never comes out on top and costs an utter fortune, he is somehow good at his job and he retained the overwhelming support of the written and broadcast media. No equivalent country or ambitious premier league team would go near him. If he was an Australian national cricket or rugby league manager with this record, he would have been out on his ear a long time ago. So why do we persist with him? Why do we think, as with the NHS, that simply pushing on in the same old way will lead to different outcomes in the future?

Maybe we are just daft. But it seems more likely that the cumulative effect of years and years of NHS propaganda has left an indelible impression. Because it would be heretical of the BBC or any political party to attack the NHS fundamentally, no debate is allowed. Indeed, when a recent SNP study in Scotland even mentioned the idea of an alternative model for the NHS, the idea was stamped on at once by Nicola Sturgeon:

"The founding principles of the National Health Service are not up for discussion," the First Minister said. "It's democratically elected governments who decide the policy basis of the National Health Service."[5]

She also referred to the NHS being funded by general taxation as a no brainer. So that is that then. No debate, no future. Keep on painting the walls in the hope that it will stop the building from collapsing. *Government decides*. Not the public, not doctors, and certainly not the patients.

There is little in the way of consumer choice for patients in the NHS, or performance related pay for staff. As healthcare consumers, we get what we are given, whether it be excellent or awful, or, as it mostly is, somewhere in between. The ideal private hospital is full of patients, as this is in the interest of those who run the hospital. The perfect NHS hospital, on the other hand, is an empty one. The staff are paid either way, and all healthcare targets are likely to be met. Consider, too, all that *capacity*.

Yes, you may love the NHS, but do you love it so much you would not pay for private treatment if you could afford it? If you needed a semi-urgent operation for a painful condition and going private was an option, would you take it? And if you believe this would compromise your principles, then consider if the same situation pertained to your child, or an elderly relative. If you had the choice, what would you do? Unless you are *very* ideological regarding the NHS, you would surely go private. And this is the point. Most people have a non-ideological approach to healthcare. If care is of good quality, fast and free at the point of delivery, does it really matter who the provider is: private, public, or a bit of both?

The other problem with a free, taxpayer-funded service is that there is no incentive for the consumer to use the service responsibly. This is because a centrally funded system will, by its very nature, always rely on self-rationing, hoping people do not take more than their fair share. In NHS primary care this means patients need to take a bit of responsibility. Coughs, colds, and sore throats do not require a visit to the doctor, yet these minor ailments still form a large part of the primary care workload. It can be frightening if your child is unwell with a fever. In years gone by, extended family members were in reach and Auntie or Granny would be able to help with reassuring advice. But multi-generational families living in close proximity have become rarer, and we now also have the internet and *Doctor Google*. Children are often brought into doctors' waiting rooms (where they are bound to catch something else from the spluttering masses) with the lightest of coughs, tummy bugs and fevers.

Modern medicine is evidence-based and evolves constantly, as is the *delivery* of healthcare. Many countries change and improve their healthcare models over time, adapting to changing circumstances and incorporating ideas from other countries. The exception is the UK's publicly funded healthcare system. Despite overwhelming evidence of patchy performance, the centrally planned structure has barely changed since nationalisation in 1948.

This 'we know what's best for you' approach is wearing thin. The best educators, teachers, and professors, see their students as equals. Treat people as if they have an assumed intelligence and they will equal and surprise you.

The public are nowhere near as unimaginative or as unintelligent as the media and the soft-left establishment that now dominates the UK would have you believe. There are many ways to have a National Health Service, rather than the current British version. Our health service could, rather than being in the hands of professional politicians focused only on the short term, be run intelligently and locally. Maybe then we would be able to retain more of our staff. The exodus abroad of British-trained doctors and nurses, who will always be in demand, is deeply worrying and has exacerbated a staffing crisis, worsening the already-low morale that drives so many to move abroad in the first place.

It is not as if we will be able to recruit from abroad for ever. We are a country in a huge amount of debt. Over the last fifteen years, we have become poorer in *per capita* terms than much of Europe, the USA, and the emerging economies of Asia. Why on earth, in twenty years' time, would any middle-class Indian doctor, Filipino nurse, or Romanian pathologist want to up sticks and leave their home to come and work in a rainy decrepit island with an ageing population, an entitlement culture, and an obesity problem?

We cannot afford *not* to train enough of our doctors and nurses. When the labour dries up from the above countries, who will we be able to entice over? The only ones left will be from very poor countries in sub–Saharan Africa, whose skills are desperately needed in their own countries, thus raising further moral questions regarding recruitment of medical staff from abroad.

The central argument of this book is not necessarily that 'privatisation' is the answer. In fact, privatisation means different things to different people, as I will discuss in a later chapter. Indeed, any change to the NHS that has private sector involvement is instantly labelled 'privatisation' by the hard left. (The idea is then attacked *ad hominem*, without it ever being clarified what it really means). For some, it may mean a more mixed system, whilst for others it equates to a sell-off of the NHS redolent of what happened to some other public utilities during the Thatcher era.

In this sense, 'privatisation', as well as being political suicide, would be extremely logistically difficult, and would simply change the ownership of the NHS without reforming it. A public monopoly and all the weighty baggage that goes with it would be replaced by a faceless private shareholder monopoly (as the NHS makes up the huge bulk of UK healthcare provision). And, even if this were possible, it would be unlikely to solve many of the day-to-day front-line problems of the NHS. The government would still retain a role as regulator and ultimate arbiter, such is the hyper-politicised nature of the system.

The privatisation of water is a salient example of how things can go wrong with an overtly ideological approach, with water companies investing poorly in reservoirs and sewerage systems, and the whole focus being toward making as quick a profit as possible. This does not work well for water and certainly would not work well for the NHS. Nobody would advocate a system that prioritises profit over basic patient care. Certainly, we do not *have* to advocate such a venture capitalistic model of healthcare, as many other counties get by perfectly well with humane and civilised private/public systems that are based on common sense, fairness, and efficiency, without putting money in the pockets of the pinstripes. Centralised socialism and healthcare by credit card are not the only games in town. There are plenty of other options between those two extremes.

We need to get away from the idea that central government should fund, run, *and* deliver healthcare. It simply creates too many perverse incentives, vested interests, and a lack of oversight. How can it be right that the same entity that owns healthcare also oversees its delivery?

This is not to say that intelligent, industrious governments can never make a difference. During World War Two, the US government mobilised its industry so effectively that it churned out a battleships every fourteen days, creating the most powerful fleet in the world in just a couple of years, displacing the Royal Navy and ensuring Britannia would never again rule the waves. But Franklin Roosevelt's governments were full of can-do men of action and excellent administrators that make the current UK government and opposition look like pygmies by comparison.

The needle of public opinion has been devilishly difficult to shift, such is the entrenched position the NHS holds in our national psyche. Astonishingly, recent polling has even showed that the public would prefer the NHS to an alternative system, *even if the outcomes under an alternative system were shown to be better*. In other words, even if the NHS is worse, people would rather keep it[6].

More government, especially *poor* government, is not the answer. Our answers lie overseas: we need only be open-minded enough to embrace them. This will be the main thrust of the second half of this book. But we must, firstly, see how the NHS myth was founded, how in is fetishised in the media, and how politicians have weaponised it. Only in this way can we have any hope of understanding the NHS Delusion.

PART ONE: THE NHS

Non Nobis Laboramus – 'We Labour Not for Ourselves'

- *Motto of the Liverpool Medical Students Society*

"I enjoy talking to you. Your mind appeals to me. It resembles my own mind except that you happen to be insane."

- *George Orwell, 1984*

1. PROPAGANDA
Trying to split the Reds

If there is one area in British life that remains beyond any widespread criticism in the media, it is surely the NHS. The broadcast media seems to operate a self-censorial culture regarding any criticism of the service, with the BBC a particularly bad culprit when it comes to hand-wringing and virtue signalling. Sky News is not much better.

Then we have the print media. Not much to expect here from the tabloids in terms of sophistication: their deliberately limited vocabulary over simplifies matters, resulting in a failure to encourage an atmosphere of real dialogue, debate, and examination.

The left-wing broadsheets, the *Guardian,* the *Independent* and, increasingly, The *Times,* are beholden to this last shining example of state socialism. They seem almost to celebrate the way the NHS has forced its way into the hearts and minds of the public at large, thus ensuring its model may be only doubled down on, rather than reformed.

We are left with the *Telegraph* and the *Spectator*. Both these publications do, in parts, show evidence of the penny having dropped. There are a handful of brave journalists who are prepared to question the NHS, but even their Martin Luther-like heresy is not enough to leave more than the teeniest pockmark on the armour of the greatest endeavour in healthcare known to mankind.

A few years ago, I was recommended Adam Kay's *This is Going to Hurt* by a colleague[7]. This book sold millions of copies, and purports to tell the story of the life of an NHS junior doctor in diary form. While I did not find it as funny or original as expected, the author did have some success recreating an NHS hospital existence: the life of rotas, fatigue, and relentlessness. The main writing of merit came at the end, as he movingly recalled the incident that caused him to quit.

After a few chapters, I already suspected we were in for a real dollop of obligatory, self-congratulatory NHS-love, and so it proved. Bear in mind that the book is constantly regaling us with stories of how low pay, poor quality of life, institutional misery, and a lack of pastoral support caused the author to quit the NHS. Surely, he would conclude the NHS is deeply flawed and want to change the system?

Not a bit of it, and roughly halfway through the book, out it came. *He would always feel tremendously proud to say he worked for the NHS*. Followed by a page and a half of gush about how wonderful and irreplaceable it all was, and how he was proud he 'did his bit'.

Seriously? I have worked with hundreds of colleagues in both hospital medicine and primary care and only very rarely did anyone mention how 'proud' they are of the NHS. They are too busy. They just get on with it. The NHS is the only training vehicle for doctors in the UK, so saying how good or bad it is, or how it makes you fill with pride (or despair) is neither here nor there.

Again, we get the insinuation that if there was no NHS

to 'look after us' there would be no healthcare at all. As if no other system could possibly be as good. As a former junior obstetrician, you would think he would know UK child mortality ranks thirty-fifth in the world, worse than almost every other major European country[8].

We also get a page of lazy and ill-informed comparison to the 'horrifying' US system, followed by a bizarre rant in favour of the NHS, using the example that private hospitals cannot deal with serious obstetric problems if they occur. Well of *course* they cannot if a monopoly provider (the NHS) takes almost all the funding. There is no incentive for private companies to compete with hugely expensive PICUs (Paediatric Intensive Care Units). Private hospitals are not equipped to deal with these cases not because they are evil, but because of the NHS, which so dominates the healthcare sphere that private medicine in the UK is forced to exist on a rarefied periphery, especially outside London. Private obstetric care costs so much because of the huge indemnity liability obstetricians take on. Insurance rarely covers private maternity due to the overheads and potential for huge pay-outs, and because the NHS is there as a taxpayer funded alternative.

Unlike Adam Kay, I have experienced obstetrics as a parent in both the NHS and a private hospital abroad. The medical care was much more consultant-led and personal in our private hospital in Singapore, where we felt far safer and more reassured.

At the end of the book, the reader gets a blast of 'the NHS is on its knees', and the nerve of an ill-mannered letter from the author to the Secretary of State for Health, lecturing him on how wonderful NHS doctors are (there was a junior doctors' pay dispute at the time).

Many of the problems with pay arise precisely *because* of the way NHS is set up. In a normal job, you would get time-and-a-half or double pay for working unsociable hours. Good luck with that one in the NHS. And it is precisely *because* the NHS is centrally funded and run that the Secretary of State is involved in an argument concerning doctors' pay in the first place. Should not pay levels be decided by the hospitals themselves, or at a local level, or even on an individual basis, as is the case in almost every other country in the world?

When you get this sort of stuff coming at you, especially when it has clearly been shoehorned-in retrospectively, you are forced to recognise it for what it is: propaganda. Either the writer is sincere, and you are being lectured to, or they are disingenuous and using NHS-love to sell a book. Be cautious, especially if the author is an ex-doctor and no longer working for the NHS he professes to worship. Be even more cautious when the BBC gets on board and turns the book into a TV series, as happened here. I was going to watch it for research purposes, but I just couldn't face it.

The colleague who originally recommended his book is a private GP. She would not use the NHS unless at gunpoint, but even she was drawn in by its sensibilities. There seems to be a mentality of *'we all know it's ramshackle and a bit useless at times, but it's been part of our lives for so long, and it is, you know, nice to know it's there for us when we really need it'*.

But is it there when you really need it? Thousands would differ from this point of view. The NHS seems to belong with good old Yellow Pages, J.R. Hartley, Auntie Beeb and Valerie Singleton, or climbing the cobbles to get the loaf of

Hovis. Nostalgia is all very well, but if the service is poor by contemporary standards, and access difficult (even when ease of access is supposedly its main virtue) then what is the point of it? Could it benefit from an upgrade? Even a faithful old Sixties mini needs more than just a lick of paint.

Since the publication of *This is Going to Hurt*, Adam Kay had doubled down on NHS-love, even making a career out of it. More books, all on similar themes, have followed.

One book, edited by Kay, was called *Dear NHS*. In it, one hundred of the great and the good of British life each provided anecdotes about how wonderful the NHS is. I am sure many of them were sincere, but as for the editor? Please God, someone make him stop.

Wouldn't it be interesting if someone published a book with a collection of awful experiences from normal patients (as opposed to wealthy celebrities)? The sort of people who do not have the financial means to jump a waiting list, or see a private doctor on the same day.

I have had personal experience of being uninsured in a foreign country when something goes wrong. It is a horrible feeling. To have to worry about money when you are unwell is awful. The mistake is to assume that the NHS is the only way such situations can be averted. Healthcare systems all over the world show us this is not the case.

Evolutionary biologists often say that religion is the result of brainwashing and indoctrination of young minds. Give me an eighteen-year-old, they say, raised in an education system absent of any religious instruction, with parents who never discuss religion at home, and present them with the two theories of evolution and creationism. Which one they would gravitate towards as the more likely? We know the answer. Creationism would be dismissed as ridiculous.

The same would apply to a comparison between healthcare in the UK and Singapore, for example. Years of indoctrination, coupled with the warm, fuzzy glow of patriotism and nostalgia, cloud the mind. But I am convinced that most people, were they to come at the choice from a completely unbiased background, would choose the Singaporean system in a heartbeat.

A few years ago, Michael Moore, the obsessive, left-leaning documentary maker, released a film criticising the insurance-based health provisions in the USA, entitled 'Sicko'. Watching this is a real education and I heartily recommend it, although possibly not for the reasons Michael Moore intended. We are often spoon-fed garbage by the British media about how the US populace is crying out for a single-payer system and evil Republicans, deride 'our' NHS as 'socialised medicine'. *What a bunch of idiots those Americans are*, we are supposed to think.

The first part of *Sicko* is a general critique of the US system. It focuses not so much on the people without any insurance at all, as those who, though they do have insurance, cannot get cover for life-threatening conditions, thus setting in motion a conveyor belt of misery, despair, and bankruptcy. One cannot help but be touched by some of the stories, however selectively they were chosen. The US healthcare system certainly has its fair share of problems, and some of them are heartbreaking.

Yet what is really fascinating is the fantasy idea held by Democrats on the left, exemplified by Michael Moore, as to what state-based provision of healthcare entails. The second part of the documentary sees Moore travelling to Canada, then Cuba (to get cheap medication), and then, finally, onto

Europe, that land of honeysuckle, socialism, and state social security that Moore somehow believes the US is desperate to emulate (even if most of its citizens do not know it yet).

This is where we depart from reality. Talk about heavily edited and highly selective! In London, Moore visits a hospital, and, before leaving, asks where he can pay. He is directed to a pay counter, where the staff pay him for some issues regarding his parking. Wow, that's socialism? *People pay you*? What's not to like? This may have come as something of a shock to the English in particular, who are frequently ripped off with sky high parking charges outside NHS hospitals.

As if to provide some degree of intellectual or political back-up for his hobby horse polemic, Moore interviews a famous British politician and makes a colossal unforced error. Naturally looking for a centrist moderate viewpoint, he interviews Tony Benn, of all people, that Corbynite superhero. Here we are told, unhelpfully, though accurately (and indeed depressingly), that there would be 'riots if the government of the day ever tried to abolish the NHS'. Full throated endorsement by the hard left tends to repel more people that it attracts in British public discourse, but again, not when it comes to the health service.

The film demonstrates the blind spot left-wing Americans have when it comes to the NHS and state provided healthcare in general. The scandals and disasters of the private healthcare system are held up as evidence of the private sector's lack of compassion, its lack of benevolence. Yet the fact remains that, although you would never guess it from watching Moore's film, the NHS has scandals too. Unnecessary deaths and maternity ward investigations. Mid-Staffs, a scandal in which people were actively killed by the system. What about the scandals of people stuck on trolleys outside A&E, or those whose ambulance calls do not result in a visit until the patient has already died? What about the (ever worsening) scandal of long waiting lists and delays in care, the one that has persuaded more British people to pay more out of pocket for private healthcare than ever before, in addition to the increasing numbers taking out private insurance?[9]

The BBC's selective reporting regarding the NHS does not contribute to open and honest debate. It neutralises it. No debate can get off the ground. As a result, with this terror of the US medical system, no mainstream politician of any party, including the Conservatives, have recommended it as a system we need to emulate. Is the right wing of the Tory party simply keeping its cards close it its chest, or does it genuinely not want to copy the American system? Which possibility is more likely?

More to the point, the lack of reasoned debate and suppression of discourse means that most members of the public, and, it should be said, the medical profession, have not got a clue how the Americans system works. I have studied it, and it is a mess of contradictions, varying from state to state, a postcode lottery with poor people and the disadvantaged being let down by the system. This is discrimination, pure and simple. Remind you of anything? The American system is more like the NHS than we care to admit.

To advocate the US system instead of our own would not be especially sensible. The system has myriad flaws: it can cause bankruptcy through healthcare bills, one flaw the UK system does not have (although the NHS, through poor or delayed care, is also capable of causing bankruptcy and loss of income). Two more reasons the US system is rarely emulated: its enormous administrative costs, and its generally poor outcomes when measured on a population basis.

The US public are very unsure how they would rate their healthcare. Some studies show high satisfaction, whilst others show that less than half of the US public are satisfied with their healthcare[10]. At the time of writing, satisfaction in the UK with the NHS is twenty-nine percent[11]. There may be parts of the US system we should copy, such as the excellent diagnostics resources, cutting-edge technology and treatments, and their huge 'not-for-profit' medical facilities, but to adopt the system as whole would be inadvisable, especially when there are other models that are less expensive, with better patient outcomes and levels of satisfaction.

Since the COVID pandemic there have been a virtual logorrhoea of healthcare books, often written in memoir form, detailing the lives of medical and nursing staff under pressure. NHS-love is always a nice way to sell a book: it is not only rather 'endearing', it also (presumably) allows the author and the publisher to feel immensely virtuous and morally superior.

This is best indicated by the way the NHS is mentioned (always in acronym form, similar to KFC) even when it doesn't need to be. 'The Covid pandemic through the eyes of an NHS nurse', 'the busy NHS junior doctor', 'Dr X works as a consultant in the NHS'. Why does this need to be mentioned? Would medical and nursing staff in other countries shoehorn in the name of their employer, or medical system? Probably not. Think of 'the COVID pandemic thought the eyes of a busy ITU nurse in southern Germany' or 'the busy hospital doctor working in the outskirts of Paris'.

Then turn the phrase around to say the following: 'the COVID pandemic through the eyes of a busy private UK GP'. Thinks how wince-making this would be. It immediately has pejorative tones, doesn't it? And who would buy it based on recent publicity?

Consider a letter that recently appeared in the travel section of a Sunday paper. The letter was an unremarkable query about flight refunds. What was remarkable was the opening sentence: 'My husband I are both medical consultants recently retired from the NHS'. Why not simply write: 'we are both retired doctors'? To ignore for a moment the professional one-upmanship implicit in the mention that they are both consultants, why do we need to know they are recently retired from the NHS? Is this supposed to be *moral* one-upmanship? It certainly reads that way, as if the fact they worked for the NHS makes then even more entitled to a holiday refund that the next person. I am sure this is all unconscious, and that there was no intention to be morally or professionally superior, but it does read that way.

Many medical books contain NHS propaganda, masquerading as virtue signalling. Another book that demonstrates this is *Breathtaking* by Rachel Clarke, a palliative care doctor[12]. The book was a *Sunday Times* Top Ten bestseller, and is a first-hand account of the problems encountered during the first wave of the COVID-19 pandemic in early 2020. This book is far less problematic than some others on the market. The author can write, for one thing, and seems genuinely honest and well meaning, especially concerning her anecdotes of front-line care, unlike the borrowed and crude anecdote by post-it note style that *This is Going to Hurt* foists on an unsuspecting public.

But wait. A few 'amber' warning signs can be found in the blurb: 'a compelling account of an NHS doctor in the midst of the greatest public health crisis in living memory'. Again, why do we need to be told she is an NHS doctor? Does it give the story any more weight? Would 'front-line doctor' be more appropriate? Again, there is the suspicion that adding the NHS acronym gives more heft, or more worthiness to the account, for reasons many healthcare professionals from overseas would find difficult to understand.

Though the book is well-meaning, there are problems. It does not take long before NHS worship pops its head above the parapet. After a heartfelt prologue, we come to the credits for the book, in which Clarke writes: 'there is one thing above all I have learned this year and would like to sing from the rooftops. The NHS rose to the challenge magnificently'. She goes on to write: 'I have never been prouder of, or more humbled by the NHS and its people'.

This is difficult to process. The NHS did not, in fact, rise to the challenge 'magnificently'. It closed its doors to non-COVID care with disastrous consequences, and, on a day-to-day basis, performed poorly, both in its messaging, lack of PPE, lack of a proper plan, and badly organised staffing. The frontline doctors and nurses in the NHS almost certainly *did* rise to the challenge. But this was despite the NHS, not because of it. In the same way that COVID successes in the UK, few and far between though they were, occurred despite the government, not because of it.

Staff took on extra hours, went the extra mile, and worked themselves in to a state of burnout, as I am sure they did in lots of other countries. I am certain that many Italian, French, German, Spanish and American doctors also worked their backsides off, but this has nothing whatsoever to do with the NHS, or the supposed uniqueness or moral superiority of our COVID performance.

The second sentence quoted does not bear scrutiny, either. 'The NHS and its people'? What does that mean exactly? In the same book, we are told how the appalling excess death toll from COVID in the UK was among the highest in the world (this was early 2020 remember). And why, pray, was that?

Do publishers insist that any medical book should have NHS love smeared all over it? Does a final draft get returned to the author with comments in red ink in its margin, such as: 'How about a bit more NHS love here?' Perhaps this helps sell copies, and helps readers to feel good about themselves, whilst also putting the author beyond moral reproach?

Also present in *Breathtaking* are the usual complaints about 'underfunding'. Yet again, we have criticism of the government's handling of the pandemic. When considering the inconsistent delivery of PPE equipment, Clarke bemoans the fact that the Government seemed to have learnt so little about infection control?'

Of course it hasn't! Why would you expect it to? Why do we rely on the 'government' (a nebulous term when applied to healthcare delivery) at all? It has proved itself utterly useless. The more involvement government has in frontline healthcare, the worse the outcomes. This is true from both points of view regarding the COVID-19 pandemic. If you are of the pro-lockdown opinion, as this author clearly is, dismissing those who opposed facemasks as having a 'furious libertarian tendency', then the thumb-twiddling and lack of leadership of the government should have put you off state involvement in healthcare forever. Conversely, those who opposed lockdowns and restrictions should also despair in the face of mixed messaging, ludicrous tier systems, and the destruction of non-COVID healthcare for no good reason.

This talk of NHS pride is baffling to many frontline health professionals, as real doctors simply do not talk like that, certainly none that I have met. They may truly *want* to believe the NHS is the best thing since hot-buttered toast, but it would be a pretty strange doctor or nurse who went around the wards or GP surgeries articulating this sentiment, and for every one that does, there are probably five others who keep quiet, thinking: 'I can't stand this anymore', 'life is too short', and 'should I emigrate to Australia after all?'

All the same, this is a book written by a well-meaning and decent doctor, with no axe to grind. There are books out there with much more of an agenda, and written with a more jaundiced pen. One such book is *How to Dismantle the NHS in 10 Easy Steps,* by Youssef El-Gingihy, a GP in East London[13]. This thin volume could easily be dismissed as obscure, if not for the remarkable plaudits and testimonials received from well-known reviewers on the left, including Noam Chomsky, Jeremy Corbyn, Ken Loach, and John Pilger. This collection of hard left, anti-western, and markedly anti-British figures should tell you all that is needed regarding the content of the book, yet the book itself is surprisingly mainstream in its beliefs and morality, at least in the context, which is that all debates about the NHS in the UK are held on the left. The centre and the centre-right do not even get a look in.

The author uses the introduction to flutter a couple of shy eyelids towards the NHS, which, we are told, 'has long been the envy of the world', and is being broken up into an insurance-based system along the lines of the US model (utter nonsense). He lets the cat out of the bag slightly when he says that this is all about much more than the NHS, instead being more about 'turbo-charged neo-liberalism', which is of course the real target.

The hard left could not give a flying toss about whether the NHS works or not. They are far more interested in fighting ideological opponents, irrespective of the fact that openness to ideas from across the political spectrum may improve healthcare outcomes. They are aroused by the huge centralised power that government dominated healthcare systems give the state over its citizens, and try to tap in to the NHS's popularity (or at least the indoctrinated terror of any alternative) by posing as its defenders.

And this is only the first page. If you can make it to the end of this mercifully short Socialist Worker pamphlet masquerading as a proper book, you can enjoy endless rants about PFIs (Public Finance Initiatives), a scheme that both left and right already concede may have been an expensive mistake (a mistake made by a Labour government, by the way). We have a few selective graphs, a few efforts of argument by anecdote, and some breathtaking assertions in the place of facts.

We are told, for example that 'NHS marketisation experiences demonstrate that markets *do not work well in healthcare*' and that 'this is clearly demonstrated by market-based health systems internationally'. This is clearly false: there are mixed systems in Europe, the Far East and Australia that all have far better outcome than the NHS.

Apparently, private providers cut costs (and therefore quality) by cutting wages, as they are not bound by a national wage structure and staff. That is completely untrue. In fact, they usually pay more, and the pay (unlike in the NHS) can be more flexible, and even be performance-related, which the hard left hates. And why cannot pay be determined locally anyway?

El-Gingihy also writes that 'private providers are accountable only to shareholder profits unlike public ownership'. These is a deliberate falsehood. The NHS is not accountable to those who use it in any meaningful sense, even if the public can be described as 'owning it'. Public ownership involves very little choice in our healthcare and almost no autonomy. You cannot take your business elsewhere, because in almost the whole of the UK, apart from parts of Central London, the NHS is literally the only game in town. You will have what you are given, chum, and if you don't like it, two fingers to you.

Accountability could, arguably, exist in a public service, in that if the service is both provided and funded by the state then it is the state, in this case the government of the day, that is responsible. But in this case, patients' power rests solely in their democratic vote. Which fact is rendered completely pointless if every UK mainstream party has an almost identical policy on healthcare and the NHS, namely that it needs more money and should not be reformed. This a case of ideological belief (Labour), intellectual cowardice (the Conservatives), and a vapid mushy cluelessness (Liberal Democrats). Even UKIP completely supported the NHS. So no, the NHS is not accountable to those who use it, at least not in any meaningful sense.

It is true, as the author attests, that the (thankfully brief) Corbynite interregnum provided some clear electoral red water between Labour and the other parties, but even under Corbyn, as we will discuss in another chapter, there was not much between him and the Tories on the NHS.

The first point in his sentence also deserves some scrutiny; 'private providers are accountable only to shareholder profits unlike public ownership'. 'Private providers', by whom I assume he means those independent of the government, are *not* automatically responsible only to shareholders for their profits. For a start, a lot of them do not have profits, because they are run independently of the state by non-profit organizations. This is true of the Netherlands, Germany, France, and many other providers all over the developed world. Even some of the largest medical centres of excellence in the US are run as non-profit institutions.

It is assumed that public ownership gives an automatic benevolence that non-government ownership of any stripe cannot hope to compete with. This is nonsense, and certainly is not reflected in patient experience or outcomes, both of which are largely absent from this left-wing rant.

The book closes with El-Gingihy's own ideas about how to 'save' the NHS in five easy steps. Number one is: 'value health and social care professionals'. Is that it? Motherhood and apple pie are nice as well, I am told. And isn't the sky blue and the sea green?

Number two: 'reverse privatisation'. Not easy when privatisation is ill-defined, and by any rational definition, is not going on in 'our NHS', certainly not when compared to many other countries. There is also the bold assertion, backed up with no evidence whatsoever, that 'a publicly run, funded and accountable NHS is far more cost-efficient than the current marketised system'. Oddly, he directly contradicts himself a few pages later by stating: 'The NHS should not simply be run by either the state or the market', which sounds like he had a moment of clarity that vanished as soon as it arrived.

Dear me. The point he is trying to make again and again, (supported, I do not doubt, by a large proportion of the political class, and certainly by a large chunk of the Labour Party), is that the problem with the NHS is not that is it too centralised or socialist in its management and delivery, but that it is not centralised or socialist *enough*. But given that the publicly funded model of the NHS is already an outlier among systems of healthcare delivery in the developed world, it takes an awful lot of brass neck to attack the NHS from the left.

But to re-enforce the point, the political left, as well as left-wing journalists and commentators, are not attacking any NHS baby steps towards the market because of any perceived effects on its performance, nor are they actually interested in outcomes. Instead, they support a fully socialist NHS on *ideological first principles*.

The point I will continue to make is that ideology and dogmatism are very bad ideas in health care. Empiricism and lived experience are far better starting points.

There is a glaring contradiction in the central critique of El-Gingihy's book. The governments of the last couple of decades, New Labour, the coalition, and the Conservatives, come in for constant criticism. It should come as no surprise that the governments of the day are going to formulate health policies, and run the NHS based on their own priorities and manifesto commitments. But the arguments being put forward are for *more* centralized control and more public ownership, which would give central government *more* power over the NHS, not less. This would seem to be at odds with the criticism that the Tories (for example) are running down the NHS. They would not be able to interfere in such a way in a more independent service, which one would assume would be a good thing. The contradiction is explained by the realisation that state control by government is desirable, only if that the government is a socialist one. In other words, we want the NHS to be in state hands, but only if it is in *our* hands.

The last few points the author makes are barely worth repeating. There is more anti-PFI ranting, and then the mask is dropped completely and he simply advocates for a Corbyn Government.

The longest serving health secretary of recent times was Jeremy Hunt. Hunt's time in the health brief was not particularly distinguished, but it was not a complete disaster, either: the fact he is pilloried by the likes of Adam Kay means he must surely have gotten something right.

At the time of writing, Hunt is the Chancellor of the Exchequer, and is busy raising taxes on hardworking families and destroying Britain's economic competitiveness with punitive corporate tax rates. His time as 'custodian of the NHS' (ghastly term), has led him to write a book called *Zero*[14], which is, ostensibly, about the need to cut out basic mistakes in the post-pandemic NHS. Hunt was a loud and enthusiastic advocate for locking down the country (and presumably the non-COVID NHS) for as long as possible during the pandemic, yet the book contains no recognition that this has made the aim of his book that much harder. In reality, the book is more an attempt at political rehabilitation.

Again, the dust jacket blurb causes those 'amber' lights to start flashing: 'The NHS is the Pride of Britain', it reads. And the author biography contains the saccharine line: 'he lives in Godalming and London with his wife, son and two daughters (all proud NHS babies)'.

What kind of nonsense is this? 'Proud NHS babies' – what does that mean? That Hunt (a very rich man) deliberately held back some of his millions to have the kids on the NHS? Or that those children, now grown, look back with pride that they were born in the NHS? Do real people think like this? They do not.

To give Hunt his due, however, a decent chunk of the book is pretty good on medical mistakes, why they happen, and what could be done better. Where he fails is in his worship of the NHS, a sneaked in assertion dressed as fact, along with a failure to grasp that it is the system itself that is clearly the root cause of many of the problems.

Most of *Zero* does indeed deal with errors and failures. Some are unique to the NHS, whilst others are prevalent in most major healthcare systems. His basic errors, whether deliberate or accidental, come at the beginning and end of the book.

In the introduction, on literally the first page, we are reassured that this is *not* going to be a book that seeks to upend the status quo or suggest anything radical. We get, naturally, some misplaced praise for Aneurin Bevan, giving him credit for creating the NHS, 'our most treasured national institution, described in poll after poll as the single biggest reason people are proud to be British'. Oh dear.

Worse is to come, however. Hunt goes on to write: 'The NHS has stood the test of time because the values it stands for have become entwined with what it means to be British'. There is some truth in this, although not in the way Hunt thinks. The NHS does indeed represent modern Britain, in the sense that it is a socialist public service, heavily dependent on immigrants, whose staff go the extra mile from keeping the whole structure from falling down, despite poor pay and conditions and abuse from the public. The NHS has stood the test of time because the public have been brainwashed into thinking there is no alternative; partly because politicians are too terrified to do anything about it (Conservatives) or are in denial of reality (Labour).

The following line reads like pure parody: 'we are proud that whoever and wherever you are – rich or poor or young and old, north or south, you can always get the healthcare you need'. This is patent nonsense.

If we have in the UK stumbled upon a uniquely virtuous mode of healthcare delivery, we should let the French and the Germans and the Australians know about it as soon as possible. But why would they be interested? What is more compassionate than excellent healthcare outcomes, which they have far more of relative to us? It is often pointed out that almost nowhere in the world has the NHS been copied wholesale. There is good reason for this.

He then briefly deals with critics of the NHS model, saying (rightly) that in any private system there would have to be a trade-off between access and equality, as the private sector does not have the incentive to put patients first (again – 'private', he fails to grasp the multi-payer's model prevalent in similar counties in Europe, where public and private healthcare often work in tandem, and where private healthcare is often 'not for profit'). He then dismisses this by saying he profoundly disagrees with advocates for other systems, yet again pointing to the brilliance of British science and the NHS during the pandemic, all without elaborating on any of it. This is not good enough.

With contributions to the debate as vacuous as this, even from Conservatives who have experienced high office, there is little hope for radical change in the future.

A better effort, not least because it is written from an unsentimental angle and is not self-serving, is the book *Life Support* by Michael Ashcroft and Isabella Oakeshott[15]. Unlike the syrupy NHS praise in Hunt's book, here (at last) is *some* acknowledgment that the NHS may not be all that good, really, and that public perceptions are very difficult to accurately ascertain, buried as they are in propaganda and wilful misrepresentation by politicians.

Sadly, while still in the introduction, the book manages to trip over its own feet when it announces: 'By way of a plot spoiler, we are not going to recommend that the NHS be dismantled, privatised or funded in a completely different way'.

Therefore, by accepting the NHS model of funding for healthcare delivery, the default approach of this book accepts Bevan's socialist model. The authors do make the slightly weedy excuse that 'there is simply no public or political appetite for change of this nature'. This is surely contestable, especially in the light of the NHS meltdown post-pandemic.

The correct way of putting it would, surely, be: 'there is not *yet* enough appetite'.

It is sad that the book undermines itself at the beginning, making its arguments much less interesting. It is sad when journalists and authors with no skin in the game, ones who could afford to be adventurous, simply piggyback on the public sentimentality and propensity for self-congratulation regarding the NHS.

At the end of the book, the authors write that: 'in the NHS this country has something truly extraordinary. Its existence and principles and the dedication of those who work for it are rightly a tremendous source of national pride'.

The NHS certainly *is* extraordinary, in that it requires staff working extra hours to prevent the whole system from going belly up. Perhaps it *is* a quite amazing sense of duty to the idea of the NHS that results in this devotion.

By simply assuming that the NHS model is the correct one, all these books fall into the same trap. Some advocate reform from the 'left' and some from the 'right', but they are all frighteningly short on specifics.

In this chapter, we have examined some of the propaganda that makes informed debate so difficult. In later chapters, we will explore other funding models that exist abroad. But the chief message of this book is the *delusion* of NHS efficacy and healthcare delivery itself. The non-ideological approach is to start afresh, looking at areas in which other countries are doing things so much better than we are. No model should be off limits, if it works. The debate as it stands, which is between the status quo and a ridiculous caricature of the American system, is getting us nowhere. The point we need to address is the NHS Delusion itself, recognising it for the sentimental and slightly embarrassing thing that it is.

2. CLAPPED OUT?
Tales from COVID

Before discussing the COVID pandemic, I should make it clear that my observations of the NHS and the performance of the British Government are an outsider's view: I was eight thousand miles away, in Western Australia. We were lucky in WA in that our experience of full lockdowns was more of the short, sharp variety, with the main inconvenience (not an insignificant one, in such an isolated part of the world) being an inability to travel internationally, and indeed between states. I cannot imagine the utter misery of months of hard lockdown with no obvious end in sight. I did experience the fag-end of the last major UK lockdown in the late spring of 2021, when shops and pubs were just reopening, although people were still being asked to sit outside, for no obvious, evidence-based reason.

At the beginning of the pandemic, countries reacted in different ways to the perceived threat. Initially, the virus was a Chinese or South-East Asian problem, which then became a Southern European problem, particularly an Italian one. There did, however, seem to be a few basic tactics in dealing with the crisis. I list some of these below. They are not mutually exclusive, as many countries practiced more than one:

- Use of non-pharmaceutical interventions, or mandates on an individual scale, such as masks and social distancing.
- The shutting down of all non-essential economic activity (hereafter known as lockdown).
- Isolation of cases and contacts, with varying degrees of strictness.
- Use of an effective test and trace system.
- The prohibition of large gatherings, known as super spreader events, such as weddings and football matches.
- Complete closure of borders.
- Quarantine or other restrictive measures at borders.

Often an overall pattern or set of priorities can be ascertained from the approach used. Rightly or wrongly, China's zero COVID approach has only recently ended. Australia and New Zealand also pursued a zero COVID approach, at least until the widespread availability of vaccines. Sweden's approach was an outlier in Western Europe, as it did not shut down its economy to the same extent, relying far more on informed consent than legal restrictions to enforce the direction of policy. South Korea, Singapore, and Taiwan, partly due to previous brushes with similar viruses, operated a highly effective test and trace system that kept mortality very low.

The one western country in which the health system and politics are subsumed, the UK, also the one country where politicians have almost complete control of the heath service, would, in theory, be expected to mount a highly coordinated and effective defence. But the British response to COVID was so all over the place that it seriously damaged our international reputation, and the perception, however unfairly, of our health service.

The view that follows is very much a personal recollection of the pandemic, and is obviously not definitive. There are plenty of books about COVID out there. What was done well and what was done badly will be debated for years to come. I am only mentioning the pandemic in the context of the premise of this book.

So, what happened in the UK? Well, initially, nothing much. The Prime Minister missed several COBRA meetings at the start of the pandemic and failed to take it seriously, which, given he was a completely unserious politician, is hardly a surprise. While this was happening, there was no talk of closing borders, as this was deemed likely to be ineffective. The measures taken by China and a couple of other countries in Asia, such as lockdowns, were thought impossible, as our open society would never accept such curbs on personal freedoms. As mentioned, some countries, such as Taiwan, South Korea and Singapore fell back on their test and trace systems, in addition to border controls. Indeed, we were told by the PM that a 'world beating' test and trace system would shortly be riding to our rescue.

Australia and New Zealand, and, amazingly, even the US, were watching us closely to see what we did next. This was, perhaps, because we got clobbered with COVID before them, or perhaps because we share relatively similar legal systems and open societies. European counties not in the epicentre of the first wave, such as Sweden, decided to adopt the same approach as the UK, centred around voluntary guidance and test and trace.

Then, in March 2020, several things happened to knock the UK government off course. One of these was the evidence emerging that COVID could be passed asymptomatically, rendering the pandemic very different from influenza. Another factor was the news coming from Northern Italy, a densely populated area with an elderly demographic, where hospitals were being overwhelmed, and decisions being made on who should be treated and who should not. Then, startlingly, a team at Imperial College led by professor Neil Ferguson developed modelling that showed there would be half a million COVID deaths in the UK[16]. As a consequence, a supposedly libertarian PM with a huge majority, under pressure from the media, panicked, as did other politicians and the healthcare establishment, and shut the country down.

Of course, lockdown in a western country is a very different beast from its Chinese cousin. People were not spot-welded into their homes, fed through their letterboxes, or dragged into ghastly field hospitals when they lay on beds like plague victims. There is only so much shutting down governments in free societies can do. Millions of workers are essential, from lorry drivers to supermarket workers, doctors, nurses, police, and the fire brigade. In this context, it was always questionable how effective lockdowns were going to be.

It was also surprising how many people adapted their behaviour anyway, a factor not considered by Imperial College modelling. All of which begs the question: were lockdowns really justified at all?

The real disaster was to be found in the NHS. Not that

the NHS *itself* was at fault. Instead, the fact that its structure was under control of politicians proved to be its undoing. Hospitals were emptied of patients, and, despite the insistence of the Health Secretary to the contrary[17], many of the elderly were sent back to care homes with inadequate testing. This is the modern-day equivalent of sending black rats covered with plague-infested fleas into towns in the Middle Ages as a form of biological warfare. The results were predictable.

Aside from Intensive Care Units, many hospitals became quieter than any of the staff could ever recall. At the PM's early press conferences, the same mantra started to emerge; *stay at home, protect the NHS, save lives.* The key order that concerns us is *protect the NHS.* Was it protecting the NHS to close down the economy, temporarily choking off the very taxes that pay for the service? No country after all, made itself healthier by making itself poorer. Many people were asking *why* should they protect the NHS, when the NHS should be protecting them?

The historian David Starkey made an awkward but surprising piquant observation when he compared the NHS to the Catholic Church[18]. When church leaders were faced with a torrent of complaints of the most appalling kind, such as crimes involving abuse of children, they had essentially two choices. Do they protect the institution, or the victims? Surely, they would not take the side of the priests? But of course, they did just that. They closed ranks and protected the institution. The victims could rot.

The Government decided that the NHS must be protected at all costs. There must be no people in corridors on stretchers piling up outside A&E (which happens every winter in any case), no impression that things were out of control, and to hell with all those old people in care homes, and disabled people, for whom face to face therapy or surgery were vital. The government could have chosen to protect the public, or at least come up with a compromise. It chose to protect the NHS, at all costs.

Even worse was to come. Shortly after the start of a lockdown that was supposedly to last only three weeks, the PM himself became ill with COVID-19 and was admitted to hospital, temporarily unable to govern. Next, the Prince of Wales was infected, and some celebrities even died, thus adding to the sense of impending national doom. Perhaps this really was something completely unprecedented?

The business of government went on, of course, and it was left to the cabinet to govern on Johnson's behalf as he received oxygen in St Thomas's hospital. Unfortunately, part of the PM's *modus operandi* was to surround himself with relatively weak colleagues, all the better to prevent or stifle any threat to his authority. His was not a Thatcher, a Blair or even a Cameron cabinet, with big hitters; this was one of the weakest groups of careerist politicians for decades, perhaps ever. So inevitably a vacuum ensued at the heart of government, a vacuum filled with lightweights such as Dominic Raab and Matt Hancock.

As the weeks went by, it became clear that there was indeed a public health crisis, with ITUs close to being overwhelmed, and the overnight pop-up 'Nightingale' hospital being put on standby with much fanfare (even though many in the NHS wondered who on earth would staff it). The daily death tolls skyrocketed, the numbers being broadcast in alarmist fashion by the BBC and others.

The public was, generally speaking, supportive of the harsh measures, and was remarkably compliant; indeed, the public were already enormously modulating their behaviour before the lockdown was officially announced. The official view was that lockdowns were completely necessary, a view that persists to this day, partially due to the huge vested interests involved. The establishment were hardly going to turn around and say, 'whoops, we got that wrong', or admit to having destroyed the economy and millions of children's education for nothing. Some commentators, lone voices in the wilderness, were highly sceptical, pointing out that the numbers of COVID cases had already begun to fall before the lockdown was announced, but they were sidelined and subjected to astonishing vitriol[19].

Then two things happened. Firstly, it become clear the virus affected old people disproportionally, in the same way as seasonal flu does. Younger and more active people noticed that if, and when, they or their friends got COVID, it was little more than a bad cold. They began to change their behaviour accordingly, acting more loosely around COVID rules and regulations.

Once again, the government panicked. Needing to keep the public in line, they doubled down on a project fear that made anti-smoking adverts seem like Peppa Pig posters. Billboards shouted 'look him in the eye and tell him COVID isn't real', with a picture of an actor on oxygen in a fake ITU bed. This ignored the fact that very few people were actually denying the *existence* of COVID. Instead, they were merely questioning the proportionality of the response.

Those scientists brave enough to question government tactics, and query whether it was a good idea to destroy the community's mental health and ability to exercise, put businesses out of work, and most importantly, ask if shutting the NHS down for routine work was really a price worth paying, were demonised in the press and subjected to disgraceful abuse on social media

The problem with the scientifically illiterate politicians, health officials on the public payroll and their television cheerleaders, was their reliance on bald statistics, COVID 'cases', 'hospitalisations' and 'deaths', rather than examining what a 'case' actually meant. A case could, in fact, be a completely asymptomatic individual. Likewise, a 'hospitalisation' could be a situation in which a patient caught COVID after being admitted for something utterly unrelated. With 'deaths', if a person was run over by a bus within twenty-eight days of testing positive for COVID, then this would be counted as a COVID-related death.

As the pandemic became quantifiable, the numbers became everything, as did 'following the science'. As 'science' is rarely settled, this became the art of following one strand of the science, the one which provided the most pessimistic outlook. This 'science' called for the most draconian restrictions possible, partly to keep the numbers down, but also to justify the seriousness of the pandemic (and therefore the supposed proportionality of the response to it). This orthodoxy spread beyond the pandemic to the NHS itself, which was co-opted by the government and weaponised for its own purposes, include the North Korean style 'Clap for Heroes'. There were *real* heroes out there in this period, overworked ITU and A&E staff, but the NHS has always had heroes (if the definition of a hero is someone who works longer and harder in the call of duty to keep the show on the road).

The media, especially the broadcast media, seemed to lose all grip of reality, taking the government line as gospel, with blood curdling and awful predictions of impending catastrophe. OFCOM even created rules forbidding the public to even hear an alternative point of view if it deviated from government advice and 'NHS best practice'.

Even *Private Eye*, whom one would expect to land a few anti-establishment punches, went 'full lockdown' over COVID in its 'health' columns. Their healthcare columnist 'MD' even now manifests as a lockdown apologist, unable to reverse tack on lockdowns, masks, and other restrictions, preferring instead to blame any pandemic errors on Boris Johnson for not locking down soon enough.

The Labour Opposition chose not to oppose lockdowns, instead demanding even harsher measures, though these would have had a much greater affected on poorer people, which demographic, one would assume, forms the core of their supporters. The Liberal Democrats, who, having redefined the 'democracy' bit to their name after the Brexit vote, set about traducing the 'liberal' bit as well, were also sucked into the 'save the NHS' quagmire. The Scottish National Party, that great bastion of principle north of the border, seeing a huge opportunity to present the case for independence, went on a wartime footing; its ridiculous leader basking in the glory of daily press conferences, using the free coverage to distinguish herself from the UK Government on pathetic points of difference, such as the timetables for lifting restrictions, and pedantic mask-wearing in certain situations.

At times, the statistics looked awful. The reputation of

the UK and the NHS was in ruins. We looked like a bunch of incompetents, getting almost every major decision wrong. Then something else happened. As soon as it had peaked, the daily total of deaths dropped hugely, leaving behind a large statistical spike. Very tentatively and slowly, the government relaxed the restrictions and crossed its fingers, hoping that the summer months would provide some respite.

Yet there was little time to draw breath. In late 2020, our very own home-grown variant, 'alpha', took hold, leading to yet another spike of infections, this time in winter, when the NHS often struggles to cope. ITU capacity and the NHS being overwhelmed were once more trotted out as reasons to do without freedoms, as if civil liberties in the UK ought to be directly linked to the NHS's ITU capacity.

Yet what had been done to prepare for the winter upsurge? Had supplemental training been given to hospital doctors? Nope. Virtually nothing had been done: we were still at the mercy of the virus. Having been stung by acting too late last time, the government and media and NHS bosses went into overdrive and overcompensated.

Whilst closing borders may have made some difference at the beginning, it was rather pointless at this late stage. Nevertheless, the government decided to start introducing immensely complex 'traffic light' systems for international travel, as if punitively destroying the travel sector was a key 'net zero' government priory.

Ludicrously, the first green list mostly included countries that had already closed their borders, with the only real tourist destination of note, Portugal, soon being pulled from the list after an upturn in cases (which was totally illogical, as the case numbers were still far lower than those in the UK). Meanwhile, the completion of a bureaucratic 'passenger locator form' was being trumpeted by Matt Hancock, who proudly sported, all the while, his rainbow NHS badge. Hancock warned that that ten-year prison sentences would be handed out to those who deliberatively chose to mislead on these forms. When it was pointed out to him that this sentence was longer than that usually given for rape, he refused to back down, insisting that he would make 'no apology' for the harsh measures[20].

That is just one small example of the huge number of infantile, pointless and idiotic rules that were introduced, making life a misery and destroying businesses up and down the country. Examples include having to wear a mask to go to the pub toilet, being unable to sit on a park bench, and, most ridiculously, the need to sit down to a 'substantial meal' rather than just a drink. All without a shred of evidence that any of this nonsense saved a single life or made an ounce of difference to public health.

The jury may be out on the effectiveness of masks in preventing transmission, although recent analysis show they may make little difference[21], but evidence shows that mask *mandates* probably do not work. Analysis of such mandates in the devolved UK nations and across the US states showed poor correlation with infection rates or deaths[22], yet politicians seem wedded to them to an almost obsessive degree. Huge assertions and claims were made for masks during the pandemic, often by politicians desperate to find anything to keep the numbers down. It is clear that, even without great evidence, politicians resorted to the attitude of *every little bit helps,* thinking, 'let's just do it then, whatever', and deciding, subsequently, to morally shame anyone who disagreed with them.

Procurement of Personal Protective Equipment (PPE) in the UK turned into farce, with hundreds of thousands of items of kit being bought from Turkey, all on the strength of a phone call from a Turkish T-shirt manufacturer. The equipment was later found not to meet UK safety standards[23]. Whether the government, Public Health England, or the NHS itself was responsible, hundreds of thousands of pounds of taxpayers' money was wasted. It was even reported that the 'desperate' NHS received some PPE from a doctor-nurse fetish site[24].

Some private hospitals were taken over by the NHS. The director of one private hospital, whom I know personally, could not *believe* how much money the NHS offered to requisition the hospital for three months at the height of the crisis. As a result, the private hospital, despite being almost empty, ended up being more profitable than normal.

NHS hospitals were also half empty, with forty percent of beds unoccupied. Routine surgery was cancelled, causing misery to patients with far more serious conditions that COVID-19. A friend of mine, an orthopaedic surgeon, was telephoned by a private colleague who asked how he was coping with the extra stress. The surgeon pointed out that there was little to do, so he and his junior staff spent most days in the doctors' mess playing pool. Is this woeful organisation and waste of taxpayers' money what people were clapping for each Thursday?

Certain aspects of the NHS *did* come under attack from the media, however, especially GPs. Primary Care staff were given all sorts of conflicting advice, initially being told to do as little face to face treatment as possible, and resort to telephone triage. The result was a huge amount of pent-up demand, so that when things (glacially) returned to normal again, they were overwhelmed. To keep some sort of grip on the floodgates, some persisted in this model, as otherwise many staff would simple have left due to the pressure. The media then hammered the government until it started issuing edicts demanding that GPs see patients face-to-face, even though that is what they were (partly) doing anyway.

Indeed, as soon as the government realised the media was directing its anger towards GPs, they jumped on the bandwagon, demonstrating exactly the kind of scapegoating that front line healthcare professionals have come to expect.

As a side note, which of the following do you believe?

A. GPs are basically lazy, do not care about patients and do not really want to see them, so they hide behind a telephone triage system as an excuse to do nothing.
B. There are not enough GPs to cope with the pent-up demand, and the system is overwhelmed, so, rather than subject patients to huge waiting times, telephone triage is used when most efficient, not out of choice, but out of necessity.

If you think we have plenty of GPs, then clearly the first option may hold some appeal. But we do not. We are *thousand*s of GPs short, and those that remain are working flat out. I'll write that again, so it sinks it.

There are not enough GPs.

Rather than being about saving lives, government restrictions were more often about saving the face of public officials, who were perpetually terrified of being accused of 'not doing enough'. Patients who desperately needed treatment for problems that ranged from mental health issues to cancer were sacrificed at the altar of COVID. The government made it clear it would protect the NHS at all costs, and they meant it. But it remains to be seen, as the death toll from other untreated illnesses skyrockets, whether the public will conclude that this was a price worth paying. Only the next few years will tell. As the horror of waiting lists of over ten million begins to bite, the NHS's reputation may be damaged in the eyes of the British public, just as it has been damaged internationally, almost beyond repair.

At first, the British public's confidence in the NHS was apparently unshaken by its performance during the pandemic. However, the consequences of this disaster will be with us for years and years. The post-pandemic period is seeing the NHS being tested as never before, and some sections of the media are at last starting to ask questions.

In December 2020, the vaccines arrived. Too late, as it happened, to save certain politicians, including the Health Secretary, who was, naturally, eager to take credit for something that had absolutely nothing to do with him. Soon enough, 'Don't kill your granny' Hancock was caught in a passionate embrace with a woman who was not his wife, and was forced to resign. He then apparently walked out on his wife and kids without missing a beat, hopefully never to be heard of in public life again.

The early vaccine roll-out was seen as a success and somewhat rehabilitated the UK's international reputation, despite political wrangling over the homegrown Astra Zeneca vaccine. Yet the vaccination program worked precisely because politicians realised it was far too important to be left to the NHS. Instead, the health service was bypassed, and, in so far as the roll-out involved the NHS at all, it once again relied on staff going above and beyond, and on a welcome army of volunteers.

Despite this initial success, enthusiasm was tempered slightly by the realisation that multiple boosters were needed, and that transmission was not affected. These facts almost saw the country plunged into another lockdown when the 'Omicron' variant emerged. The variant was initially discovered and sequenced in South Africa. For their honesty, the South Africans were rewarded by almost all counties (as the UK had been over 'alpha') with another pointless travel embargo. As more information became available, studies showed that, despite increased transmissibility, the variant was 'extremely mild', and that Western countries really had nothing to worry about[25].

The messages coming out of Whitehall and Number Ten were infused with yet another round of panic. Despite the positive news coming out of South Africa, the Chief Medical Officer, Chris Whitty, immediately announced that of 'what we do know so far about Omicron, everything is bad'[26]. It was not. Whitty, in this instance, was either misinformed, ignorant (which is worrying in a pandemic), or being deliberately misleading – but to what end?

Masks were back, the hospitality sector was essentially put on notice that it could be closed at any moment, and yet more colossal damage was done. Many in the cabinet were on the verge of initiating another Christmas lockdown, until they were threatened with a backbench revolt of massive proportions.

Although climbing down, the government decided (just for good measure) to unleash *another* round of jabs in record time, to be carried out by heath care staff and volunteers, which they could then take credit for. That way, if the number of hospital admission went up anyway, it could be blamed on members of the public who had not come forward for their boosters.

The chief problem with the leadership of the NHS during the pandemic is that there wasn't any. On one hand, there was Boris Johnson and the hapless Matt Hancock, and, on the other, Patrick Vallance (Chief Science Officer) and Chris Whitty. Whilst the scientists could simply hold up their hands and say: 'we are only advisors; advisers advise and ministers decide'. Politicians, meanwhile, could retort that they were being 'led by the science'. This was not leadership, and it blurred the line between elected officials and professionals. What it meant, in the final analysis, was that *nobody* was in charge.

As time has passed since the end of the COVID-19 pandemic, more evidence has become available regarding the performance of the NHS. The most sensible indicator is not the number of COVID-related deaths, but the number of excess deaths over a certain time period. Despite everything, the NHS was remarkably average in its performance compared to other countries. Most of the clangers were dropped by the government itself. The one true success was the early and rapid vaccine rollout, that even the wretched Johnson government realised it could not trust to public sector administration.

So, the performance of the NHS was so-so. About average. And if you are now thinking: 'oh, that's all right then', I would once again refer you to the opening premise of this book.

Middling mediocrity is not good enough. If the performance of the NHS was not actually that bad, the performance of the government was appalling, and should be a lesson in the unwanted consequences of statism. Unable to get to grips with the soft butter of a virus, the government decided it 'had to do something', always a worrying motivation. Into the vacuum of their own inadequacy, they poured a huge litany of rules, creating a huge amount of misery and long-term damage. All of this reached its nadir in a ludicrous tiered system, one that entailed regions of the UK being treated as if they were in different levels of the prison system.

The material damage done by this nonsense will be reflected in damaged education, mental illness, and unnecessary cancer deaths. It was an illustration not just of the failures of the government in the sphere of health, but of the failure of government intervention *ad hominem.*

The late Christopher Hitchens challenged his audience to come up with a way of causing the most possible damage while using the least possible words. His best response was 'condoms cause AIDS', a phrase uttered by Africans Clerics (goodness knows how much misery *that* caused). While possibly not quite in the same league in causing direct deaths, the phrase 'social distancing' is equally catastrophic, and caused all its own damage using just two words, rather than three.

It is true that many Western countries were unprepared for the speed and severity of the outbreak, yet few had the UK's lethal combination of a lack of protective equipment alongside slow, badly organised testing. You may wish to blame the government, rather than Public Health England or the NHS, for not acting more quickly, and for failing to heed warnings. But was the disastrous outcome purely due to the government? Were Public Health England, or the wider NHS, *completely* blameless?

Many partisan points were made in the UK, arguing that the reason we coped so badly with the coronavirus pandemic was NHS underfunding or 'austerity', but this is not the case. During the years following the global financial crisis, the NHS budget was ring-fenced by the Conservative/Liberal Democrat coalition, and its spending allowed to rise in real terms year on year[27]. The increases were smaller than previously years, but represented a country teetering on bankruptcy and trying to live within its means, rather than some cruel plot to destroy the NHS.

Even as late as the 2019 election, there were many differences between the incumbent Conservative administration and a far-left opposition, but throwing money at the NHS was not one of them. During the last decade, a hypothetical Labour government would *not* have spent significantly more. I am no fan of the modern Conservative Party, but on this one issue it is, at least, consistent: give the NHS as much money as possible, but do not bother to reform it.

When criticism of the response did take place, journalists zoomed in on the small parts of the NHS that are private, or contracted in from outside, ignoring the elephant in the room. If you are ideologically committed to a centrally run service that does not work properly, it is easier to criticise the peripheral details, thus avoiding bigger problem.

The public need to decide the level of government involvement it wants within the NHS. If you take the view that the government are all idiots and the NHS would be far better without interference, then great. If politicians are useless at running the NHS, let it be independent. But the NHS in its current form cannot be *wholly* independent. It is essentially a socialist system that relies on central planning. You cannot have it both ways. If you want a health system provided solely by the state, you must accept the state being involved in running it.

The British can be innovative and ingenious when it comes to expertise and planning. The 2012 Olympics were a triumph of organisation. British businesses and the public at large are generally good in a crisis, or in exceptional circumstances. Those bits of the NHS that functioned well in coronavirus were the ITU units themselves, and Critical Care Staff, who, from what colleagues tell me, did brilliantly. GP surgeries also rapidly adapted to different ways of working, such as telehealth, with a real team ethos and sense of collaboration amongst practices. This is exactly what you would expect from a set of small businesses, contracted to the NHS, but able to make front-line decisions locally. These are the front-line staff that people should be clapping, not the chaotic health service they work for.

As to the idea that the NHS is the envy of the world, this crisis was the final nail in its coffin. Other countries looked on in disbelief at our performance, struggling to understand our celebration of a health system that had performed so poorly. *Nobody* will be studying the NHS as a health system any time soon, unless it is a study in failure.

A real post-crisis inquiry should look at the current structures and demand urgent reform, but I fear we are further away than ever from this happening.

Prospective patients were terrified into staying at home to protect a health service that should have been protecting *them*. Hospitals were emptied of elderly patients, who were discharged into care homes. Care homes are not part of the NHS, so the COVID-19 care home crisis was presumably a price worth paying. Clearly the government thought so, doubling down on the myth of the infallibility of the NHS, with the full-throated support of the BBC and broadcast media, who were only too happy to pump out round the clock virus TV, a sort of 'project fear' on steroids.

The Prime Minister even boasted that the NHS had been protected by a 'human shield'[28]. Is that a price worth paying? Surely not. This was a monumental disgrace, and must never be allowed to happen again. When you put the health service ahead of patients, something is rotten at the core.

Looking abroad, Germany's health system coped superbly with the COVID-19 outbreak[29]. Mass testing was rolled out rapidly, with public and private sector labs working in harmony. In the UK, private laboratories offered their services but were told, rather sniffily, that they were not needed. Private GPs who procured coronavirus tests were threatened with court action for profiteering.

At the time, Germany spent two to three percent more on health as a share of GDP than the UK[30]. Most of us would be happy to pay more for a better quality of health service, even via tax increases, but surely less happy to cough up extra money to paper over the cracks of an unreformed NHS.

Singapore's response, meanwhile, was highly effective, resulting in reduced rates of infection and the avoidance of a UK-style lockdown. When a second spike came along, it was due to a uniquely Singaporean factor: an outbreak amongst guest construction workers from the Indian subcontinent, who were staying in dormitory accommodation. An unforeseen problem, but you can bet your life Singapore will learn from this, and that, if there are further outbreaks of novel viruses in the future, these dormitories will receive much closer scrutiny.

Australia and New Zealand followed an approach that led to very few deaths[31], far less than those in other Western countries. In fact, New Zealand's approach even led to 'negative' excess deaths (meaning that less people died than would usually be expected to in a given year). This was probably a consequence of less mixing and spreading of illnesses like the flu.

The approach of these countries was to completely close their borders and shut themselves off, forbidding their own citizens to leave. Only a small, controlled number were allowed to return, and even then at the expense of strict quarantine isolation: returnees were not allowed to leave their hotel rooms for two weeks. In Australia, even *state* borders were closed, separating loved ones and damaging businesses.

Of course, viruses are perfectly capable of evading even the strictest measures, and some spread took place regardless. When it did, and case numbers began to rise, extremely strict lockdowns were imposed, far harsher than those in Europe. Vibrant cities such as Melbourne spent months with the life being throttled out of them and saw the police arresting, and in some cases beating, members of vulnerable groups, such as the elderly, and, in some cases, pregnant women, all for minor infractions[32].

The approach (utterly unapologetic by the way) of these countries was only possible due to their extreme geographic isolation. With hindsight, it may appear to be the correct strategy, but there are three major flaws in the 'Zero COVID' approach.

The first is the immoral closure of borders, damage to families, and destruction of livelihoods.

The second is that, in order to achieve 'Zero COVID', the closure of borders must remain in perpetuity. The population is isolated; low rates of COVID cause very low levels of natural immunity, resulting in a population that is hugely susceptible to a 'wave'. To open the borders, reduce restrictions and allow free movement would mean the whole strategy was a waste of time. The only circumstance that could ride to the rescue was the development of a safe and effective vaccine. As we now know, vaccines *were* developed, but there was no guarantee of this happening, making the whole exercise a huge gamble. If the vaccines had not come along, these countries would still have closed borders, and sporadic severe lockdowns, to this day.

The third objection is the moral implication of waiting for vaccines, which must be developed and trialled in countries with prevalent COVID in the population. So, the Antipodean countries relied on other countries to develop the vaccines, which they would then purchase. New Zealand did not develop anything, and Australia's only serious attempt at a vaccine was abandoned after it was shown to cause erroneous HIV positive tests[33].

Essentially, the approach was, 'you guys can all live and die with your COVID, and when you come up with a vaccine, we will buy it off you, thanks very much. And as we are relatively wealthy, we have got sharp elbows. So, to hell with third world counties such as India, who need the vaccine more urgently, we will have it ourselves'.

I find this approach morally problematic, but the leaders of these countries were completely unaware or unmoved by any ethical considerations. Mark McGowan, the premier of Western Australia went nuts for COVID zero, openly bragging about the low rates in his state, seemingly unaware that his lockdowns and border closures were ruining lives. Millions could be put under lockdown because of a single case. Puffing out his chest and insulting anyone who disagreed with him, he boasted of defeating COVID. Good luck with that, mate. Still, he won re-election, which was, of course, the important thing.

Other states hardly covered themselves with glory, with the health secretary of South Australia telling people not to handle balls at football matches, and to beware of pizza containers 'because of COVID'[34]. This was worse than a parody, and showed a new risk-averse Australia, far removed from the rough and ready frontier country in the British popular imagination.

COVID caused a lot of public officials to lose touch with reality completely. It comes to a pretty pass when, during the height of these ludicrous restrictions, and downright embarrassing tiers and lockdowns, one ends up agreeing with David Icke, the reptilian humanoid conspiracy theorist and loon. His appearance in Central London rally, gut bulging under his shell suit as he set about bellowing anti-lockdown rhetoric through a megaphone, was something to behold.

It was interesting that the poster pin-ups of the left, Nichola Sturgeon (former SNP leader), and Jacindia Ardern (former PM of New Zealand), who championed shutting down their countries and trampling on civil liberties, barely lasted a year once the pandemic was over and real politics returned. They each saw the writing on the wall and got out quickly, saying that they had 'run out of battery', when, in reality, they were going before they could be pushed.

It seems that having a good pandemic does not, in the end, cut you much shrift in the real world.

3. GENESIS
The Creation Myth

Everyone knows how the NHS was founded. In the beginning, there was Nye Bevan. On the first day, he separated the light from the dark. On the seventh day, he could have rested, but no, he decided to create the National Health Service, and he saw that it was good.

Aneurin 'Nye' Bevan has lived on in the national consciousness far longer than other Labour politicians of his era, his reputation carefully shepherded by his ideological surrogates in the BBC and on the political left. His legacy has become completely intertwined with the NHS, and exists, therefore, almost beyond criticism. If he is not actually the Godhead then he certainly sits at his maker's right hand. Yet apart from his name, and the fact he 'invented' the NHS (which is not completely true), most of the public know very little about this rather prickly and difficult individual from South Wales.

Born into a family of ten children, not all of whom survived childhood, Bevan was one of nature's instinctive rebels, angrily rejecting authority from an early age. He developed an acid tongue and a gift for rhetoric. Having been down the mines from the age of fourteen, it was unlikely that he would have ended up a Conservative. Instead, he was seduced by the theories of Karl Marx, and dedicated himself to a unified world view. His politics remained fundamentally Marxist: when he later went into politics, he denigrated the capitalist norms of society. It remains a uniquely British curiosity that, in almost all walks of life, Marxist thinking has been either discredited or fallen out of fashion. It is never completely dead, however, as shown by some of the trade unions elites, the domination of the left at UK universities, and indeed the Corbynite entryism takeover of the Labour Party. Most prevalently, though, it lives on in healthcare, and in the lionisation of 'Nye' Bevan.

Bevan argued with everybody: employers, fellow members of the Labour Party and, naturally, Tories, for whom he reserved a deeply personal revulsion. He argued intensely with the leadership of his own party, yet when the Labour Party was returned to power at the end of the Second World War, he was still sufficiently impressive enough to be handed the Health Portfolio.

At the time, a National Health Service was already on the table, and had been accepted, to a degree, by both major parties: an NHS was going to be made anyway. The NHS act of 1946 became the blueprint for the enactment of the service two years later. What Bevan *did* do is seize the opportunity to implement the NHS as a socialist project, affecting its structure by negotiating agreements with GPs and consultants to gain their co-operation into the new system. He cajoled, bribed, and outwitted the medical profession, until they became co-conspirators in the largest expansion of the state in the UK in modern times. He also succeeded in establishing the NHS in the national psyche to such an extent that almost nobody has any idea of what came before. There is no concept of the hospitals, doctors and healthcare advancements that preceded the NHS. The general assumption is that there was basically *nothing*, and unless you were extremely rich, you were flung into the streets, to be left at the mercy of the poorhouse, or of charities. This is rather like Johnny-come-lately fans of Manchester United, who believe football started with the Premier League in 1992.

There is the assumption that without the NHS, the decades that followed the Second World War would have resulted in the sick being untreated, poor people being left to die in waves of diseases, high infant mortality, and low life expectancy. This is fine, if we are to assume that, without the NHS, there would be nothing. As most other countries have shown, however, there would not have been 'nothing'.

It is simply untrue to say that there was no system or infrastructure before the NHS. The Medical Act created the medical register as early as 1858, which at least gave the public a layer of protection from charlatans[35]. And, in the Liberal Government's National Health Insurance act of 1911, a limited form of state health insurance was introduced, although it was mainly restricted to lower paid workers.

The generally poor state of the health of army conscripts was noted during the First World War, and by 1939 the government had launched the emergency hospital (later medical) service; this had been planned for years, and had some shortfalls, but showed the benefit of good administration and co-ordination of medical services. More strikingly, in 1944 a politician announced that the government intended to establish a universal national health service, but that politician was not Aneurin Bevan: it was Winston Churchill.

At the birth of the NHS, households were sent a leaflet containing the following information:

'It [the NHS] will provide you with all medical, dental, and nursing care. There are no charges, apart from a few special items. There are no insurance qualifications. But it is not a "charity". You are all paying for it, mainly as taxpayers and it will relieve your money worries in times of illness.'

What has endured here? There now exists a whole array of 'charges', from prescriptions to parking. You are certainly not automatically provided with dental care, since dentists resigned *en masse* from the service (good luck finding one these days). NHS dental provision has been in crisis for years.

In the days of almost full employment, it was probably true that most people *were* taxpayers to some degree. Today, with millions on out-of-work benefits, the NHS, despite the best of intentions, has become a charity to all intents and purposes, being absorbed into the wider welfare state. Yes, you have no immediate money worries in times of illness, but with huge waiting times, patchy services, and poor health outcomes, you simply have other worries, instead.

Now think also of what Britain gave the world in medical advances before the NHS was founded. Think of these five medical breakthroughs: understanding and prevention of cholera epidemics, vaccinations, anaesthesia, antiseptics, and antibiotics[36]. All were developed either solely or partially in the UK. We were world leaders in mass public health long before the NHS was founded, before waiting lists and bed blockers came along. Yet we have, since then, let others overtake us.

Clearly, no system is perfect, and what preceded the NHS had gaps in its coverage, although most people, even the poor, could get some treatment. The health system did what it could, rather than trying to do too much. But when outcomes are examined, it is difficult to say which the best system is: the pre-NHS system, or the NHS itself. The NHS may have more fairness and equity, although this on its own does not necessarily improve quality of treatments. If we place equity above quality then the NHS is probably a big improvement. If the priorities are switched, however, the NHS's superiority becomes less of a given.

Once one accepts that, had the NHS not been introduced, there would have existed an alternative type of NHS or state insurance scheme, it is surely conceivable that we could have ended up with a better system than the one we have today. What Bevan did is apply a socialist, state controlled, top-down model of government healthcare, in which the state pays for the NHS via taxation, decides how and where patients are treated, and then provides that treatment. This was unheard of in the developed world outside communist countries, and remains so today, with almost no major first world country copying the NHS.

The concept of an NHS appeared in the Beveridge Report a few years before it became a reality[37]. Lord William Beveridge was a liberal politician, and certainly no socialist. There is remarkably little in his report on healthcare that we would recognise today, still less a 'blueprint for the NHS', but there was a belief that healthcare should be free at the point of need and not based solely on ability to pay. There was a moral imperative to this that was pertinent for the time: as troops came home from the war, it was believed that they deserved a safety net of health care to befit a land fit for heroes. The healthcare system at the time was not deemed universal enough; too many were leading lives of bad health that could be avoided.

Interestingly, the Beveridge report does not advocate a purely tax-financed healthcare system, but one based on the 'contributory principle'. These contributions would be defined, meaning that money that went from the patient's taxes into the NHS could be regarded as *their* money, so the public would have a direct stake in the service. General taxation was discussed only as a top-up when shortfalls arose. This model of defined contributions is similar to many current continental systems, although there is only one insurer, the state, and there would therefore be no market forces or consumer choice that could be leveraged to keep prices down[38].

Beveridge and Bevan were cut from very different cloth; the only thing the two men had in common were the first three letters of their surname. Beveridge was born in British India at the heyday of the Raj, and was subsequently educated at Charterhouse, and then at Balliol, Oxford, that soft-left training ground for politicians. He was something of an agnostic, which was unusual in his day. He also (not so unusually) had a pretty fruity belief in eugenics[39], in theory, if not in practice. But whatever Beveridge was, he was no Marxist: he saw a welfare state as very much a means to an end, rather than an ideological destination.

The Beveridge report goes as far as insisting that 'the individual should recognise the duty to be well', and that 'restoration of a sick person to health is both a duty of the state *and* the sick person'. The report also states that the 'duty' of the state includes leaving the individual free to provide more protection and more care than whatever safety nets can be guaranteed by public insurance; the individual is, too, free to take initiative and risks.

It is important to understand that the NHS need not have been organised according to socialist principles. Indeed, in the sphere of primary care, it was not (and still is not), as GP practices remain (just about) independent contractors. The reason the NHS came into being in its current form was due in no small part to Bevan's Marxism. The problem with this approach is that it is not empirical. Other healthcare systems could have been examined elsewhere, and some of the health structures in the UK that preceded the NHS could have continued, especially those shown to work well in practice. But instead, the baby was chucked out with the bathwater, and the NHS arrived as a matter of ideology imposed from Whitehall, not for empirical, practical, or moral reasons (unless you view Marxism as having an inherent superior morality, which, if you were a Marxist, you probably would).

Bevan himself ended up resigning in 1951 for, unsurprisingly, purely ideological reasons: he resigned in opposition to the NHS charging for dentures and spectacles. The Labour Government also fell at the end of that year, and Bevan spent the rest of his life in opposition, never holding a position of power again.

We will now return to the Beveridge report to examine the 'H' in the NHS. The word is there for a reason: one of the primary points of Beveridge was that *Health* ought to be the system's main objective. Treating disease is not the same as keeping a population healthy, especially as eighty percent of health is unrelated to healthcare, being more linked to lifestyle, genetics, diet, and so on. There are many things you can do that are 'unhealthy', and yet outside the remit of the medical profession. There is, for example, no correlation between how near your house is to a large hospital and your longevity; indeed, spells in hospital can have a negative effect on patients. Poor food and lack of exercise has caused many an eighty-year-old to come out of an NHS hospital a virtual invalid compared to when they went in.

The 'Beveridge' NHS is very different from the model we have ended up with, especially in its implication that a safety net would lead individuals with more ability or means to access extra provision for themselves beyond that safety net alone. Whatever this phraseology of Beveridge is referring to, it certainly is not dependence on the state. A sense of individual responsibility is present here, a refreshingly unideological approach. If the original model had been applied, it is not difficult to imagine a thriving private sector, in which those who could would insure themselves beyond the existing state provided insurance, as they do in Germany, for example. What Beveridge would have made of people's dependence, in the form of benefits and the NHS, or of generations of people living on handouts, without a single family member working, is anybody's guess. Mercifully, however, the welfare system is outside the scope of this book.

The following quote from the website 'Past Medical History' neatly encapsulates the commonly accepted view of the NHS and Bevan:

'On July 5th, 1948 the NHS was finally launched and the

Labour government took responsibility for all medical services. For the first time ever nurses, doctors, pharmacists, dentists and opticians were brought together as part of a single organisation with free diagnosis and treatment for all. The first patient to be treated by the NHS was 13-year-old Sylvia Diggory, who had a serious liver condition. She got to shake the hand of Aneurin Bevan that day and recalling the event she said: "Mr Bevan asked me if I understood the significance of the occasion and told me that it was a milestone in history – the most civilised step any country had ever taken, and a day I would remember for the rest of my life – and of course, he was right."[40]

One wonders exactly what 'of course' Mr Bevan was so right about. Was it that Miss Diggory would remember it for the rest of her life? This is surely correct. Was it the most civilised step any country had ever taken? Better than abolishing slavery or giving the vote to women, to name but two? Surely not.

It is interesting to observe that, in the build up to the 'creation' of the NHS, the medical profession were agents of conservatism, grumbling with discontent and supposedly getting in the way of that nice Mr Bevan. A bit harsh, given that the BMA proposed as early as 1930 that health insurance coverage should be given to the whole population. Doctors were understandably worried about the lack of independence over both their professional lives and their income, and wary of becoming mere public sector employees.

The decades that followed have shown their concerns to be well founded. Deference and respect for doctors have gone down the toilet, as has their real terms pay. They are now the most over-regulated group of professionals on the planet, so much so that many – sick of mandatory training, appraisals, and revalidation – retire early.

In an example of what was to come in the NHS, the predicted annual cost of its first year of operation was almost doubled. One million pounds was budgeted for opticians, but within a year the cost was over thirty million. The BMA in 1949 predicted the rate of NHS expenditure would lead to national ruin, because of an aging population and the fact that the NHS was now footing the bill for more expensive and complex diseases. You can ask yourself whether or not they were on to something.

Beveridge predicted that the initial jump in demand for GP services would eventually fall as people became accustomed to the system. This shows a charming naivety in relation to both public expectation, and the inevitability of dependence on the state.

Let us now revisit another couple of paragraphs from the 'Past Medical History' website:

An Institution Worth Fighting For

In the years that have followed the NHS has struggled through many early difficulties to become the envy of the world. The service it currently provides is nothing short of extraordinary. In the 14 years that I worked for the NHS, I witnessed the work of many remarkable individuals, whose expertise and dedication are staggering.

The formation of the NHS is one of our greatest national achievements and perhaps one of the greatest achievements in history. Returning to a private healthcare system may seem like a solution to some but we only have to look across the Atlantic to see that this is not a magical solution that will make the current problems of the NHS go away. In the US 20% of adults have no usual source of healthcare and medical bills are the biggest cause of bankruptcies. This is surely not the future we want in Britain. Just as Aneurin Bevan fought to set up the NHS, we should follow his lead and fight on for its continued survival.

This is clearly rubbish. The NHS, as we will show *ad infinitum*, and now even admitted by both the Leader of the Labour Party and its Shadow Health Spokesman, is not the 'envy of the world' and never has been, certainly not for other first world countries. The author is right in that many remarkable individuals use their expertise and dedication, but this is to prop up an NHS that falls short on so many levels.

Aneurin Bevan was no secular saint. He used a template for a welfare state, one developed by a liberal intellectual during the Second World War and, given his brief, was responsible for the enactment of it. In doing this, he departed from its original premise and, after negotiation, pushed through a socialist model whereby the state takes responsibility for the healthcare of the populace, rather than the situation of shared responsibility envisioned by Beveridge. In doing so, the state also provided the delivery of healthcare, acting as the chooser and commissioner.

The suggestion that this socialist model is a mark of great civilisation, or somehow makes us the envy of the world, is patently wrong. And the assumption that no other system could have performed a similar role just as well, or even better, is likewise mistaken. This line of thinking ignores the fact that healthcare is organised and practiced differently outside our shores, often with better outcomes. It is, in short, a delusion.

4. GUILTY PARTIES
How politicians have weaponised the NHS

Prime Minister's Questions (PMQs) was televised for the first time in the United Kingdom in 1989. The PM at the time was Margaret Thatcher. The first question concerned NHS funding and was asked by one of her backbenchers, Tim Yeo[41]. Mrs. Thatcher has attracted both opprobrium and praise in equal measure, and her detractors would certainly never think of her as a natural defender of the NHS. This makes her answer to the question surprising, as she was happy to say that the NHS was indeed 'safe' in her hands before confirming, and even boasting, that the NHS budget had risen in real terms every year over the decade of her premiership.

Was this true? It was[42]. During the Thatcher years, NHS spending did not rise nearly as fast as it would later under Blair, but it rose nonetheless. The fact this happened in a much more inflationary era is even more remarkable.

So, what gives? Wasn't the Iron Lady a brutal privatizer of the NHS? Didn't she and her evil government regard the NHS as a joke? Weren't they determined to replace it with a private healthcare system modelled on that of the United States? Well, if they did, they had a funny way of showing it. Apart from a few market reforms, such as GP fundholding, and some tentative steps toward an internal market, the NHS was largely left alone.

Why was this? It is lost on many opponents of Thatcherism that the lady herself was a far more pragmatic politician than people given her credit for. She knew her government would never beat Labour on the issue of the NHS, so she did not attempt to.

However, in contrast to the cloying outpourings of NHS-love from more recent Conservative leaders, Thatcher made absolutely no bones about the fact that she used private healthcare herself. This was presented as a virtue (*as per* Beveridge), Thatcher pointing out that those who had the means to pay should do so, thereby easing the burden on the system. It shows how far left the debate (if there is one) on the NHS has shifted, to the point where you would *never* get a Tory leadership candidate speaking in this way today, even though I know from personal experience that at least one recent Tory leadership candidate, while singing the praises of the NHS, was in fact a regular attendee of a private clinic in Central London where I was doing agency work.

The 2022 Conservative leadership election was a case in point. Once whittled down to five candidates, all were only too happy to embrace their love for the NHS, presumably too terrified to say anything else. Even a 'reformed' NHS was not mentioned, or any indication given that the extra funding promised would be properly spent, rather than simply being added to the budget.

The Conservative Party has always had a strange relationship with the NHS, despite its time in power being deeply interwoven with the development of the service. After all, the Conservatives have, since the founding of the NHS, been in office over sixty percent of the time. In theory, during this time, they were entrusted by electoral mandate with stewardship of the NHS. Yet they were, conversely, not trusted on 'Health' by much of the electorate.

The Conservatives inherited the NHS as one inherits a rather uncooperative and difficult stepchild with whom it is impossible to win favour. In the election immediately following the founding of the NHS, the Tories seemed to accept as a *fait accompli* this huge increase in the government mandate. They may not have been particularly happy about it, and the NHS was certainly more expensive than originally predicted, but, unlike British Rail, messing about with it would have been too complex and unpopular a move. It was, therefore, ignored by the party in the hope that it would go away of its own accord. This, of course, did not happen.

These were the days of post-war consensus: there was general cross-party agreement over large sections of policy. The Labour Party, more ideological in its approach at the time, had no qualms about adding to the budget again and again. It should be remembered, however, that while the Labour Party of the post-war era may have been robustly socialist in some respects, it was also rather patriotic and conservative. Although it did, even then, have a lunatic fringe that showed some ankle to the Soviet Union (in a way not dissimilar to the recent Corbynite interregnum's 'useful idiot' approach to the Putin kleptocracy).

This innate conservatism was reflected in the average worker, who had a degree of national pride, self-respect, and a quiet patriotism, none of which qualities were mutually exclusive with a sense of class grievance and a desire for fairness. This was before the expansion of the welfare state that, under New Labour and the new 'red' Tories, has now reached its apogee. For workers in the fifties, the idea that an able-bodied worker would live off taxpayers' money by choice would have been seen as akin to rewarding idleness, and would have carried with it a sense of social stigma and shame. Also absent were the feelings of entitlement and victimhood that have done so much to damage the West over the last couple of decades.

Attitudes were important, as they affected the way people used the health service. You rarely troubled the doctors for minor issues, and (horror of horrors) did not task them for help filling out social security forms, or consult them for non-medical 'life stress' issues such as relationship breakups or redundancy, in a way that has now become commonplace.

But times change. After the cultural revolution, the country became much less powerful, this in inverse proportion to the growing strength of the trade unions. As the unions had helped found (and fund) the Labour party, the party naturally took a pro-union stance. The Conservatives, almost by definition a very *non*-ideological party, were unsure quite how to deal with the unions, especially the shock troops of the NUM, and they lost power as a result.

Tony Benn said: 'The Labour Party has never been a socialist party, but it has always had socialists in it'. Similarly, the Conservative Party has always had ideologues, they have merely been far less visible. However, a small but influential strand of opinion began to emerge amongst the intellectual wing of the party in the Seventies, via Enoch Powell, spreading to others such as Keith Joseph, who underwent his own

Damascene conversion. This thread of reasoning, unlike the old Imperial or 'Union Jack' right-wing, was founded in a complete rejection of the post-war consensus and represented the first occasion since the Second World War that a genuine ideological shift had taken place on the centre-right.

When Margaret Thatcher defeated Ted Heath in the 1975 leadership election, the Conservative Party suddenly had its own off-the-peg ideology (or, at least, its leadership did). British politics has not been the same since. If the Seventies were divisive, the Eighties were even more so. A bitterness and rancour grew at the cellular level in the body politic, poisoning debate, even as the quality of that debate was enhanced by the two main parties continually pushing one another into their different spheres of belief, like two perpetually opposing magnetic forces.

Mrs. Thatcher, that Boudicca of free enterprise, began destroying the working class, slashing taxes, and privatising everything. Or so the left would have you believe. The reality was that monetarist targets were abandoned, new taxes such as VAT were introduced, and privatisations were delayed until they could be secured with further electoral mandates and better economic conditions. No PM survives eleven and a half years without a healthy dose of realism. During these years, the NHS structure was left alone. Funding did indeed go up in real terms each year, but not by a huge amount. There were waiting list and cuts in some areas, but the performance of the NHS did not noticeably decline during this period. It was pretty good value for money, if not exactly world-beating. To describe the NHS at the time as a second-rate service for third-rate levels of spending would probably be accurate.

Labour always asked for more money and even conjured up fake stories about people being forced to go private, most famously during the 1992 election. But they were in semi-permanent opposition, so there was bugger all they could do about it. The ideological shift also affected Labour, who, under Tony Blair, would not seek to undermine the Thatcherite consensus and would instead take forward existing policy on taxation and union law, abandoning any commitment to renationalisation, as epitomised by Clause Four of the Labour Party constitution.

The NHS did play a role in Labour's 1997 election win, but at the time was very much second to the 'education, education, education' mantra. Whatever one now thinks of 'New Labour', and they have been pretty demonised of late, they were at least a serious group of politicians with a good idea of what they wanted. Politicians such as Gordon Brown, Robin Cook and David Blunkett carried genuine heft and substance. Compared with the current dross on the Labour (and Conservative) front benches, they were giants. Intellectually, they were not quite on the level of Wilson's cabinet in the Sixties, nor were they blessed with the real-world business and legal acumen of the various Thatcher administrations, but they did have talent.

Little was done during Blair's first term, but, over the thirteen years of New Labour, changes to the NHS did happen. GP fundholding was abolished and replaced with a similar system on commissioning. A huge funding increase took place, and there were new contacts for consultants and GPs that finally gave adequate reward for their effort. Waiting lists went down, and new hospitals were built.

Unfortunately, borrowing ballooned to pay for it all.

Complex taxes were introduced to ensure the productive private sector was squeezed to pay for the inefficient public one. The cracks were papered over by Private Finance Initiative (PFI) contracts that would prove ruinously expensive in the medium and long term.

When the financial crisis hit, we realised, or should have realised, that we were broke. Utterly broke. Skint, in fact. Someone had to take the hit. Blair's replacement, the hapless Gordon Brown, was out. The Tories were back, after a fashion, in coalition with the Liberal Democrats.

Now that the Conservatives were back in office, the NHS began to be weaponised as never before. Ed Miliband, the new Labour leader, even admitted as much[43]. The coalition were constantly being accused by the opposition of trying to 'privatise the NHS'. This despite the new PM saying quite clearly that he 'loved the NHS', speaking movingly on the treatment of his disabled son[44]. The Conservative-led coalition also increased NHS spending year on year, albeit at a much slower rate than New Labour. But this was still not enough to slake the opposition's thirst for more and more spending, despite the country's credit card limit being long since blown.

As the years went by, the siren song continued: 'the Conservatives want to privatise the NHS' (sorry, '*our* NHS'), selling it off to the highest bidder. The opposition – apart from planning to spend more money that the country did not have – seemed to have no policy of their own. These attacks did nothing to help the Labour Party, which went backwards at the 2015 election, and probably reflected their own ideological and moral bankruptcy.

Depressingly, however, the Tories seemed to take all this

criticism on board, and an ideological conversation took place within the party in order to retain power. This was entirely in keeping with the history of the party, which sees its existence in office as being inexorably tied up with the best interests of the country at large, rather than the principled neo-liberal approach, as envisioned by the Thatcherites.

Like Labour before them, the Tories decided that electing bald, older men who would appeal only to the party base was a sure-fire way to lose elections. Electing youthful looking, fresh-faced centrists, on the other hand, would be rather a good idea. Thusly, the second great Tory ideological postwar shift happened, not straight away, but over a decade or so, accelerated by Brexit and the COVID pandemic.

This new thinking on the centre-right has seen government spending being seen as a virtue by Conservatives, a moral right, even, whilst voices of caution or financial prudence are dismissed as 'nasty'. As healthcare is naturally a very emotive part of the government's brief, trying to reduce or freeze the healthcare budget was seen as 'cruel'. Even trying to link increased spending to reform is now regarded as a moral evil. And so, we have the tedious and ideologically depressing sight of the Tories engaging in a bidding war with Labour as to which party can spend the most public money on an unreformed NHS; or, in other words, which party can throw the most taxpayers' money down the toilet.

After Labour's defeat in the 2015 election, due in no small part to their eradication in Scotland, a part of the UK that had provided the bedrock of many a Labour parliamentary majority, the party decided to elect an extremist as leader. Labour's new leader was not elected by the parliamentary Labour party, who had more sense, but by its members, boosted by a huge influx of left-wing entryists. With the election of Jeremy Corbyn, huge gulfs immediately opened between the centrist Tories and the new hard-left opposition. Differences in education, foreign policy, defence and hot button 'diversity' issues all became obvious.

But not on health.

The Corbyn rabble continued the tried and trusted 'Tories want to privatise the NHS' mantra, this time to the point of parody. Had an asteroid, during the period, ever been minutes away from wiping out all life on earth, these people would probably still have been bleating on about the Tories, privatisation and 'our NHS'. And yet the Tories, under Theresa May, an exceptionally mediocre PM, simply moved into the centre-left territory that Labour had vacated, enshrining above inflation increases in NHS funding into law. There was no debate whatsoever about value for money, outcomes, or serious reform of the system. The funding pledges in the two main parties' manifestos were so similar that they were barely an issue in the subsequent general election[45].

Corby's advocacy of the NHS being in the public sphere and deserving of almost unlimited extra funding did *not* mark him out as an outlier. On the contrary, it is a vivid illustration of the ideological bankruptcy and moral cowardice amongst all parties that he was merely articulating the consensus, even the establishment viewpoint. This is ironic, as I am sure he would define himself as an outsider. Indeed, for all the supposed radicalism of Jeremy Corbyn, John McDonnell, and (heaven save us) Diane Abbott, when it comes to the NHS, their political stance was so wholly mainstream and anti-reform that one could almost call it conservative.

But, whatever one thinks of the hard-left, they are, at least on this point, painfully consistent. This contrasts with the ideological *volte face* taken by the Conservative Party, which, in a desperate attempt to neutralise the issue of health, simply moved over to the leftist position. Thus, we have the bizarre spectacle of a profoundly non-ideological party espousing and agreeing with socialist ideology, presumably for short term political gain.

Even today, there is no sign that this consensus will ever fracture. It is not clear who the villains of the piece are, though in this case the hard-left *do* have at least a ghost of point when they claim the moral high ground, something they do with no hint of self-awareness.

Are the villains the socialists, who esteem equity and access above outcomes, and regard publicly financed and publicly-run heath care as being self-evidently virtuous, even in the light of poor performance? For those on the hard left, excellence in health may be desirable and even welcome in a socialised NHS, but it is incidental. The fundamental point is the equity of the system itself, not how well it does its job. If, somewhere, the health service fails, or is seen to fail, then there must be some other culprit, whether it is the creeping involvement of the private sector, or some perfidy dreamed up by the Tories.

This sclerotic and inflexible approach fails the public on all counts. The fear of 'privatisation' or 'selling off our 'NHS' that Labour deploys as a deliberate political strategy, especially at election time, has stymied any sensible debate for decades. Labour have persisted in this approach despite it being blatantly obvious that the Tories have no intention of doing any such thing. Perhaps it is because almost all the state socialism of the late forties has now passed into history, with only the NHS left standing. Maybe, in their desperation, Labour feel this is the only card they have left to play. Maybe they really believe it.

This makes the Conservatives possibly even more culpable, as they did not start off believing in the NHS, and even those who say they do, but probably do not, are too terrified to do or say anything radical. Even those Tories, such as the ghastly Matt Hancock, who wear NHS badges and profess their love of the system in interviews, spout this guff only because they believe it will benefit them politically. If the NHS ever does fall out of favour, expect this same type of politician to nod sagely whilst claiming to have been aware of the system's faults all along. It is rather odd that the Conservatives, despite professing to be the party of private property, low taxes, and individual freedom, have a complete blind spot when it comes to something as important as the healthcare sector.

There is certainly a sulphurous whiff of hypocrisy about all of this. But perhaps the Conservatives are simply living up to their name. It is impossible to say. A small 'c' conservative would likely not advocate anything as radical as fundamental reform of the healthcare system. But when this system is essentially socialist, it is, surely, an abrogation of duty to leave it unexamined.

When the results of the 2017 General Election became known, it transpired that a combination of protest voting and Theresa May's laughably poor campaign had almost put a Marxist poseur in Downing Street. Brexit was also a big factor. Later, May's inability to manage the UK's exit from the European Union (even trying to gain support of the opposition to push through a staggeringly bad deal) meant her party lost patience with her. She was out. Her antithesis, and some may say nemesis, Boris Johnson, then easily won the party leadership, and thus the premiership, on a simple message of completing Brexit, and/or winning a general election. Johnson (sort of) achieved the first aim, and did in fact achieve the second with a remarkably large majority in December 2019. This was the end, naturally, of Corbyn.

Then, before we had been given any breathing space, the COVID pandemic hit. Brexit, almost overnight, became yesterday's news. The government was gripped by panic and indecision when it came to both lockdowns and the NHS, on which all three main parties showed remarkable unanimity.

If Labour had previously talked about weaponising the health service, the Tories went all-out nuclear on 'our NHS'.

Towards the end of pandemic, Johnson performed a breathtaking act of political nerve by breaking a manifesto commitment in relation to the NHS. While all the criticism and talk of privatisation has come from Labour, harping on about how the NHS was in mortal peril, Johnson broke a manifesto commitment from the other direction, *increasing* national insurance to fund the NHS, under the weak cloak of a 'social care levy'. It was a cowardly policy, yet not without its political merit, as the opposing parties could hardly oppose more money for the health service: that would have gone against their repetitive Orwellian mantra.

Johnson's self-absorbed premiership was a disappointment to all. He turned out to be a one trick pony: a carapace of punchy speeches and rhetoric masked a soft underbelly, with a chronic inability to pay attention to detail and no substantive grasp of the issues facing people on a day-to-day basis. As a campaigner, he excelled. As a Prime Minister, though, he will go down, despite his election victory, as one of, if not *the* worst PMs in living memory. *Stay at Home, Protect the NHS, Save Lives.* Many will wish that Boris had simply stayed at home.

At the time of writing, the first cracks seem to be appearing in the pandemic legacy. If the opinion polls are to be believed, the public may be falling out of love with the NHS for the first time[46].

Little thought seems to have been given to the future of the NHS by either major party. As the population ages and healthcare becomes more expensive, inevitable increases in the healthcare budget will push the UK into penury. You can only borrow money or skim off the departmental budgets of other areas of government, such as education, defence, or transport, for so long. The only solution would be whopping tax rises, or the running down of the health service to the point that it eventually collapses in on itself.

No party can, surely, be taken seriously if all it has to offer is a decision to pile debt onto future generations. Short term political unpopularity must be risked: courage must be found from somewhere. Given the recent 2022 Conservative leadership election, this is not going to happen any time soon. It will certainly not be easy, but as JFK said, we want to do the great things not because they are easy, but because they are hard. Yet visionaries are, sadly, hard to come by in politics these days.

Another common refrain posed by the Labour and, to a lesser extent, the Liberal Democrats, is the assertion that there exists an evil Tory plot to sell the NHS off to the USA, or to

Donald Trump. This drivel has not one shred of evidence to support it, and must have left many Tories ministers scratching their heads in bewilderment.

It may be worth examining what exactly is meant by 'privatisation' of the NHS in any case. Does this mean a 'floating of the NHS', similar to an Eighties utility offload, in which the public would be invited to apply for a prospectus and purchase shares? There would surely be few takers, given chronic inefficiency and indebtedness of the NHS.

Or is privatisation supposed to mean that services are gradually withdrawn, until they disappear completely? This is happening now, not because of an agenda of privatisation, but simply due to the chronic overloading of front-line services that are already buckling.

In many of the practices I have worked in, Podiatry have closed their books to new referrals, as have ENT and several minor services such as ear syringing, wart removal and, more importantly, counselling and psychology. All vanished, due to being underfunded (or not funded at all), a difficulty in recruiting staff, or being overwhelmed by demand. This sort of fraying and disintegration of the service happens all the time, and patients are forced to go private, not by design but by accident. I do not believe that the system is being deliberately run down, but it is being eroded by a lack of oversight, poorly allocated funds, and inadequate recruitment. Incompetence and bureaucratic inertia in other words, rather than any coherent strategy.

The COVID pandemic should have brought the health service into sharp focus and started a debate about its future. The fact that know-nothing politicians were constantly interfering during the pandemic, warping clinical priorities (although this was already happening) with their incessant re-organisation, is surely evidence enough that governments of all stripes should be kept the hell away from healthcare. COVID was a good argument for a healthcare system that is run independently of the state, no matter what its source of its funding.

To illustrate the huge overlap between the government and the NHS during the time of the pandemic, there is no better example than the performance of the aforementioned Secretary of State for Health at the time, Matt Hancock.

When two women who were jogging and having a coffee during the first lockdown were stopped by the police for an infringement, Hancock backed the police, when in fact they were the ones acting illegally. Either way, what did this have to do with the *Health* Secretary? Why was he the one standing up in the House of Commons, issuing threats to get the public to comply with draconian nonsense? It is quite extraordinary that he involved himself in such a huge infringement of liberty in the first place, let alone that he interfered and gave his opinion on police action to enforce the more ridiculous laws.

During interviews, when Hancock was asked what he thought his job was, given the level of muddle and his demonstrable incompetence, he said: 'It is my job to save lives'[47]. No, it is not. That is the job of A&E doctors. His job is (or was) to carry out government health policy. It is difficult to imagine a European health minister describing his job in a similar fashion, but then such a person would be unlikely to have their head swimming with power in the way that Hancock's was.

And now, post-pandemic, the NHS is almost in meltdown, with record numbers of patients on waiting lists, and cancer referral deadlines being missed. This is only partly the result of the 'closing down' of the health service that took place during COVID, but that decision did exacerbate the catastrophic performance of a healthcare system already at the brink of collapse.

Going forward, it is difficult to imagine that any politician would be willing to risk unpopularity by fundamentally changing the NHS. Hopefully, the lack of satisfaction with the service shown in recent public surveys should provide an opening to those who suspect things could be done better. Years of fear mongering have made the public frightened of change, but the near collapse of the service may provide wiggle room for at least some sort of debate to be had. If we continue to see our politicians trumpet their NHS love from the barricades, however, even that may be too optimistic a prediction.

In recent years, it has become clear that any substantial reform of basic health care in the United Kingdom is far beyond either of the two main political parties. The Labour Party is in too deep ideologically to ever step out of the grave it has dug itself. The Conservative Party, meanwhile, after so many years in power, or at least sharing power, appears intellectually exhausted. It would be refreshing and inspiring to hear some new ideas for reform and improvement of the NHS, but none are forthcoming. All we hear is the unpleasant tinny sound of the can being kicked down the road, with future generations being badly let down by this utter paucity of ambition.

Often, when the media, or a protest group, or a doctors' union, points out that the system is in utter crisis, understaffed and underfunded, the news item ends with a government spokesman blandly issuing a statement saying something along the lines of: 'Mental health/GP services/emergency care staff, are one of the priorities of this government, and we recognise the extraordinary work they do. That is why we have invested (insert numbers) million pounds directly into the service to enable front line staff to increase their targets'. In this way, the government subtly deflects blame back onto the clinicians.

If those responsible for the NHS are more interested in deflection and avoiding blame than making the service better and listening to staff, then it is time for a complete sea change in the way we do healthcare in this country. The point cannot be made enough: keep politicians and Whitehall away from the health service.

The NHS-worship of the smaller parties, the SNP, the Liberal Democrats and the rest, amounts to little more than facile and vacuous virtue-signalling. The Liberal Democrats, at least, may at lionising the NHS because they really believe in it. The Scottish National Party, though, with their ugly, divisive tactics, have their own motives for everything they do, or say, a fact which should be obvious to any casual political observer.

The NHS delusion has been fed and watered by all the major political parties. Governments of all stripes have pushed the idea that the NHS is the envy of the world. Whatever one thinks about the health service, the depth of the involvement, or interference, by politicians of all shades of the rainbow has been an unmitigated disaster.

Our elected representatives, have fed the NHS delusion for short-term political gain, and are now stuck in a quagmire of their own making.

5. STATE OF AFFAIRS
Philosophy and ideology

With a few exceptions, the UK's National Health Service is free at the point of delivery. The service is provided directly by the state, unlike 'free at the point of delivery' healthcare systems in other countries which may be delivered by insurance companies, or via compulsory state insurance schemes. This aspect of the NHS is not unique. This may seem like stating the obvious, but it is an extremely important fact, given that many members of the public cite this supposedly unique aspect of the NHS as the reason for their pride in the service and continued support of it.

The founding principal of the NHS, that 'healthcare should be available to all, free at the point of delivery, based on clinical need and not ability to pay' is difficult to refute. It remains a fine principle, but the health service is not run as an abstract idea or statement, nor is it funded by motherhood and apple pie. The NHS is run by real people, often centrally by civil servants, elected public officials, or managers who have very little experience of healthcare.

'Ability to pay' is a somewhat problematic term, especially in the NHS healthcare model. Of course, ability to pay can get you quicker access to healthcare in the UK, as we have an expensive, elitist private sector. Anyone who can afford it can literally jump the queue ahead of those who cannot. The only way to stop this would be the illiberal approach of outlawing private health care provision, which would turn us into even more of an international outlier on healthcare delivery than we already are. And those who think private healthcare should be outlawed would have to answer the question: what would that solve? It would be a case of ideological purity within our shores only, as the wealthy are, of course, more than capable of hopping on a plane to Singapore, Dubai or Houston and being treated there instead.

Inequality would only be exacerbated this way, unless traveling abroad for healthcare was also banned in the name of equity. Good luck with that. Restrictions on those leaving or entering the country are a step in the direction of a police state, rather than a fanciful socialist nirvana.

Health insurance is all very well, you may ask, but what about the uninsured? Despite the existence of the NHS, the worry, in recent years in the UK, especially post-pandemic, has been the huge rise in patients paying out of pocket for healthcare[48]. In the UK, with its huge NHS waiting lists and tiny private sector, this is a particular tragedy, and one that the wider British public would normally associate with the US system. If desperate people are unable to rely on the NHS as their last line of defence, even ending up taking out loans to pay out-of-pocket for private healthcare, then surely this is more evidence of a broken system.

Most other developed countries adopt a far more liberal and non-ideological approach to healthcare, with a large private sector working alongside the state, often in partnership with it. Models have evolved over Europe in which a large healthy private sector is able to utilise market forces via competition to bring costs down, and so offer more choice for those that seek to avail themselves of their services. Do Germany, Spain, or Sweden, regard themselves as morally inferior to us? They seem able to manage to fit the square peg of state provision into the round hole of the private sector without compromising on performance or outcomes, and in the absence of any screaming from their own left-wing parties.

Hand-in-hand with a single payer government system, there is usually a belief, not based on any evidence, that healthcare based on clinical need and not ability to pay is a mark of a civilised society. This carries the inherent opposite opinion that, under a different system, a society would not be civilised. In addition, the prevailing wisdom is that the UK is also both more civilised and morally superior to the society we lived in before the founding of the NHS in 1948.

Rather than healthcare being both run and paid for by government, could it be paid for, but not run by government, as it is in the Netherlands? Are the Dutch somehow *fairly* moral and civilised, but not *quite* as morally pure as we are in the UK?

Why should the state necessarily have any involvement in healthcare *at all*? Again, the received opinion in the UK is that healthcare is too important to be left to the independent sector or the individual. But what if the reverse is in fact the case, that health is too important to be left to the state? There is a belief that the government is uniquely 'kind' or 'efficient' at delivering good outcomes when it comes to healthcare. Take a moment to re-consider this in the light of COVID-19.

Where the basics of healthcare overlap with our

environment, it seems reasonable for government to take some role. It would take the most extreme libertarian or anarchist to maintain that environmental public heath, such as adequate sewerage facilities, mass vaccinations as a form of preventative medicine, quarantine at our borders, and so on, should not be the remit of the state, for practical reasons as much as anything else.

To return to the idea that healthcare is simply too important to be run outside the sphere of the state, we should look carefully at what the state is *not* involved in. Is healthcare the most important thing in your life? Yes, one could say that you would be very restricted if you were not in good health. But most of us, mercifully, do not need healthcare every day. Most of the time, most of us are well. Visits to the doctor are not a regular part of our day, unless we have a severe disability or a chronic illness, for example. Most of us (again, not all) will go about most of our days coping perfectly well without healthcare. Healthy living and individual choices drive eighty percent of our health, while only twenty percent is due to healthcare provision[49].

Let us look at food and shelter. These are universally more important than healthcare. Without food or drink, a person will be dead in a matter of days. Without shelter, in the UK, at least, it is possible to die of exposure in just one night. Yet shelter, in the form of housing, is *not* wholly provided by the state. In fact, the majority is private. Likewise, food and drink are not nationalised at all, unless one counts the purchase of sustenance indirectly via benefits.

Socialism can provide a quasi-religious unified field theory for everything, in a way Stephen Hawking (a well-known socialist) would have approved of. The benevolence and competency of the state are self-evident to true believers. State control is believed to be the end, not the means, to higher standards and better outcomes. The aim of socialism is to secure for the workers the means of production, distribution, and exchange (the levers of the economy). Under such a belief system, it is an axiom that state control is better, and that institutions like the National Health Service must be run by the state for the benefit of the people. Good outcomes are desirable, but are incidental to the system. State control is all. Changes will only ever take the form of tweaks: there will never be any fundamental reform of the role of government in healthcare.

When the state both pays for, and runs, healthcare, you have a dangerous drift, with a lack of quality control. To snap the thread of supply and demand is inadvisable at the best of times. A situation in which the public view 'free' healthcare as not just as an entitlement, but something they should have access to at the snap of their fingers, all the while being presented with a great deal of choice (a very consumerist attitude), we have the makings of a very potent brew of dissatisfaction. The gap between what the state can provide and the public's soaring expectations becomes so gaping that it risks the entire system collapsing in on itself.

The NHS is designed by socialism according to one of its key principles: equity. Equity of access may be a perfectly noble thing to aim for, but is it the *only* thing to aim for? And should it be pursued at the exclusion of other goals, such as excellence, or choice? Apparently so, as the recently history of the NHS shows. It does not matter how far we fall behind other counties, how few MRI scanners we have, how long our waiting lists are, as long as everyone is treated the same, we are happy. In the wider economy, this can be called equality through poverty. In healthcare, it can be characterised as: 'we know what's best for you, so get what you're given and don't you dare complain about it'. Or, put more briefly: 'we know it's shit, but tough'.

I have worked locum shifts on Accident and Emergency wards, where patients would sometimes (very politely) point out they have private healthcare, and would therefore like to be referred to their own private specialist for a follow-up, rather than going through the NHS's outpatient system. Although they are essentially freeing up NHS capacity by using their own private provision, the reactions of NHS staff were something to behold. Some refused point blank to get involved, others recommend that patients go back to their GP to start from scratch, and one was told, literally, to 'piss off', as being referred privately was 'against the principles of the NHS'.

How far, I wonder, can this be taken? If everyone has a poor service with huge waiting times, premature deaths, and the inability to book a primary care appointment, at what point does it become the *system* that is at fault, rather than a reason to demand more money for something that is obviously not working for anybody?

Socialists will brook little criticism of the NHS, however bad it gets. If the Conservatives are in power, it is those nasty Tories underfunding the system who are to blame for the NHS's poor performance. If Labour are in power, then it is claimed that Labour is too right-wing, too wedded to Tory underfunding.

As was shown in the pandemic, public health is not the most important thing in life. Illiberal restrictions may (in theory, if not in fact) prolong life up to a point, but only by diminishing its quality. This feeds into the terror of death, and the general principle that prolonging life is always desirable, leading to the nonsense conclusion that a long life is better than a life well lived, and healthcare systems have a moral duty to prioritise the former over the latter. Indeed, there is evidence to show that although life expectancy has gone up, the number of healthy years we have on average has altered very little[50].

A ruinous amount of money is spent keeping the very elderly and infirm alive, with no regard to human suffering. There is surely a moral discussion to be had here, but try that in these hysterical times. As with anyone daring to question the lockdowns, the rejoinder 'so you would just let old people die, then' is the classic retort, always uttered with much venom, and it has the same argument-ending power as an accusation of racism.

The rather strange thing about socialism is the way that the converted, particularly the young, act as if they are privy to some sort of revealed truth, and that if only the thing was done properly, it would end up transforming everyone's lives for the better.

State socialism is a system in which equality and equity are both the journey and the destination. But life is not like that: there will always be things that make us unequal. Some of us are more talented, worked harder, are better-looking (sorry, life is not fair), or are more intelligent. Attempts to engineer equality of outcomes do not work, and it is surely not right to put all the levers of power in the hands of the state and hope everything works out alright. Yes, in Singapore or Norway, you may be okay, but best of luck trying this in most other countries. A dictatorship of rich arseholes will be replaced by a dictatorship of ruthless well-connected arseholes. As Michael Lonsdale says in *Munich*, all France did post-war was exchange Fascist bastards for Gaullist bastards.

'Socialism' has been an unmitigated disaster: at best, you have run down, depressing misery factories in Eastern Europe, and at worst, the Gulag and North Korea. Socialism is not the universal brotherhood of man (or woman), only a shifting, temporary alliance of self-interest, national, strategic, or otherwise. Socialism, by definition, puts power in the hands of the state and reduces individual choice and, therefore, liberty. And there lies the important point. Socialists are only too keen to point out that the opposite of their creed is capitalism. But this is a misreading of Marx in some respects. The word 'capitalism' was rarely used in a negative sense (if at all) before Marx, and even he only generally used the term 'capitalists' to refer to financiers and factory owners, rather than the middle-class bourgeoisie. Socialists, however, do not do nuance or sophistication. The genuine opposite of state socialism is, surely, *freedom*, rather than the socialists' idea of a villainous capitalism.

'We are many, they are few' is socialists' the mantra. This is fine if you are a Russian peasant living on the land, but it is not so relevant to Western European democracies with an educated and large middle-class who are capable of making life choices, discerning between ideologies, and voting in a way that reflects their values.

Anyone who supports more socialism and central planning

as any sort of answer to the problems that face the NHS, and the UK in general, should consider where the sheer attractiveness and magnetism of liberty comes from. In a reductionist fashion, you would be hard pressed to think of any socialist, panned economy that has seen a net migration flow from a freer, liberal, more market-based economy. Market economies attract immigrants, socialist planned economies provide those immigrants. T'was always thus, and people vote with their feet. Follow the footprints, as you might say, rather than following the money.

Consumers are more nuanced than socialists give them credit for. They increasingly have very high expectations of healthcare, ones that the creaking state-run NHS will be unable to provide.

Central planning does not work well in healthcare unless the end goal is *truly* universal, as previously suggested regarding public health measures such as vaccinations. The answers may lie in locally run hospitals that can grow and shrink according to local needs and local healthcare priorities. That way, the frontline NHS would be able to adjust itself according to consumer demand. As soon as you reinstate the link between supply and demand, then some planning, at the local level at least, can be considered, in the same way that all market-based interactions happen: with trust and realistic expectation on both sides. Taking a socialist centrally-planned path you get what you are given but, again, this does not take any account of the sophistication of the consumer.

Although public expectations of the NHS have soared, we may be seeing something of a reality check following the pandemic. Undoubtedly the yawning gap between what people expect of a state-run service and what it can provide has rarely been larger, and it would take a brave politician to confront this.

Politicians, being are far removed from the front line, do not have to worry about the sharp end of interactions, and the media are more than happy to nudge the blame onto NHS staff. All this results in the very people who are paid the least, and who are the least responsible for the problems, get it in the neck. To poorly fund and fail to reform a primary care service that is overwhelmed by demand and then blame the situation on 'lazy' doctors and 'rude' receptionists is quite shameful.

Ideological issues also arise in the political and wider sphere over the subject of benefits or handouts. The NHS is, in some ways, the ultimate handout, though it is not means tested of course: that would (surprise, surprise) be in violation of the 'founding principles of the NHS'.

It is typical of dependency that the patient's involvement in their healthcare journey has everything to do with illness and nothing do to with heath. Prevention, which was supposed to be a real boon for the NHS, has been lost in favour of ongoing crisis management. The conversation that no politician will have with the public concerns not just the NHS, but the 'welfare state' in general, an elastic term that seems to include all spending in the sphere of benefits, social care, and the NHS itself. This budget has risen inexorably, creating dependence on a massive scale. Although welfare may have the best of intentions, it does not always have the best of outcomes, as can be observed in the performance of the NHS, in which equity overrides excellence at every layer of planning and policy.

An unchecked benefit culture often suffocates any sense

of independence or personal responsibility. At the level of the individual, to take one example, making provision for private health care is a proactive choice that one would make as a consumer, while weighing up one's own priorities. This may be thought of as a luxury by some, as we cannot all afford private healthcare. There are two responses to this – firstly, we could easily make private healthcare more affordable, by reinstating the tax relief abolished by Gordon Brown. This may help to create more of a free market, one in which mass participation in private healthcare pushes costs down by competition.

Comprehensive healthcare would not necessarily be the goal. One could choose from a range of packages with different levels of cover. Let us consider, for example, someone who plays sports regularly: they may want to take insurance that covers them for physiotherapy or rehab due to injury. Another person may prioritise maternity cover because of horror stories at her local hospital. Whatever the reason, the complexity of human interactions and lived experience makes the individual by far the best agent to act in their own interests.

Even if taking out medical insurance is not an option for all, it is surely preferable that as many people are covered as possible. This could to create a boom in the private sector, in terms of hospitals and jobs (these of course pay tax, which could help fund the NHS). If ten people with health insurance remove themselves from a waiting list of twenty NHS patients waiting for a hip operation, then it the waiting time for the procedure would, theoretically, be halved.

But it is highly unlikely that any of this will happen in today's climate, given that the UK's politicians seem unable or unwilling to articulate that dependency, passivity and overreliance on the state are *not* a signs of healthy population. Benefit culture may slightly nudge you up from the bottom rung of absolute poverty, but goodness, do people pay for it in other ways, such as poverty of ambition, poverty of independence and, yes, *poverty of health*.

Being stuck on handouts, by accident or design, can cause people to become enervated, lacking in purpose, and more likely to become depressed, bored, tired, and obese (in whatever order you chose). You need something to get up for in the morning. Genuinely disabled patients on benefits have often expressed their amazement to me, in private, that anyone would *want* to be dependent on others, finding it difficult to understand how people can actively prefer the loss of dignity to working for a living.

The Conservative-dominated governments of the last decade or so have colluded in this nonsense, meaning that we now have an entire class of people, most of whom are able to do some sort of productive work, but are instead entirely dependent on state handouts for their existence.

Dependence may lead to extraordinary passivity in health (a dangerous thing when so much of health is improved by prevention rather than cure), not just in terms of seeking healthcare, but in motivation to carry out treatment. A proactive patient who strains their knee will be on the internet looking for exercises, and, if these fail, will contact a physiotherapist directly, or press their doctor for a referral. The physiotherapist will take the patient through a range of exercises, which, when carried out diligently, can lead to recovery in just a few weeks.

By contrast, your passive patient will do nothing at first, before eventually contacting their GP, complaining about their knee, and being referred to a physio – and what will they do then? Not much, is the answer. After an inevitable grumble about the wait, even if it is short, they will turn up at the physio expecting to be 'cured'. They will sit sullenly while the physio goes through the treatment, and then not bother with it at all, instead bouncing back to the GP to claim that 'the physio didn't do anything', or that 'the physio was useless', all this accompanied by the inevitable request for a sicknote, or 'fitnote', as it is now called.

Tackling this type of attitude is immensely fraught, from a political and cultural point of view. The choices involved, such as reducing or tapering benefits, or streamlining NHS services to essential services only, will be seized on as 'uncaring'. One thing the pandemic has taught us is that when the state hugely increases its power, pays people not to work, and gives the impression of having an endless supply of money, paring back entitlements after the fact is hugely (and depressingly) unpopular.

At times the priority given to equity within the socialist superstructure of the NHS seems to render quality and outcomes almost irrelevant; if everyone has access to the same treatment, even if it is substandard, then all is well. But think of a private system in which you could opt for an 'A' bed, a 'B' bed, or a 'C' bed (Singapore has just such a system, which we will come to later). The actual treatment is pretty much the same, but you may be seen more quickly in a 'A' bed, for example, than a 'B' bed. There will also possibly be a 'D' bed, where the care is of a basic safety net type. This concept, prevalent abroad, creates outrage in the UK, yet surely the outrage is only justified if the alternative is a system in which *everyone* gets 'A' possibly 'B' grade care. The NHS, though, based on outcomes in other developed countries, delivers mostly a 'C minus' service on average, if that. Surely, therefore, the previous system, with its ability to deliver more positive outcomes, is better than mediocrity for all.

The NHS can only be funded long-term, in its present form, by empowering the private sector to grow and pay the taxes the NHS depends on. The alternative is ever increasing taxes, or worse, hoovering up money from other departmental budgets.

But even the *word* 'private' when used in the context of health gets an awful lot of people upset. A question for NHS purists, who baulk at any private sector involvement in health: what exactly do you mean by 'private sector'? The NHS has contacts with a huge number of private companies, without which the service would be impossible to run. Hospital meals and catering, for example, are routinely contracted out privately. If private contracts were truly thought to be the root of all evil, the NHS would have to provide its own food. But where would it buy the food from? Farms, which are, of course, small businesses. What would it then do with the wheat? Have NHS workers grind it into bread? Surely not. We do not, mercifully, live in a country of collective farms, with the means of distribution being controlled by the state. Presumably you would *have* to pay the food industry to make hospital meals for the NHS.

What about equipment? Would the NHS have to make its own MRI scanners, rather than paying the private firms that make them? A ridiculous idea. What about medicines? Up to ninety-seven percent of new drugs in the last twenty-five years were initially researched and developed by the private sector[51]. Should the NHS instead be responsible for developing its own drugs? This is inconceivable, even for the most optimistic on the hard-left.

And should the NHS take back control of the GP practices that exist as independent contractors? Without GPs running these themselves, there would be a large amount of extra work for relatively little reward, and a new army of managers would need to be appointed.

An ideologically pure NHS, in a market economy, would be both utterly impractical and undesirable.

However, in the interest of balance, we should also make a case for change *from* the left, or at least look at ways in which a more market-orientated and less publicly funded system could create even worse institutional unfairness than the current NHS model. Given the overwhelmingly leftist single payer system that is the NHS, the clear red water is little more than a trickle, but let us try.

Firstly, we can acknowledge that, despite all the nausea-inducing invocation of the 'founding principle of the NHS', there are some valuable safeguards within the original premise. It goes without saying that no civilised society would advocate completely 'red in tooth and claw' medicine, a situation in which an inability to pay would get you nothing, or lead to you being 'thrown out onto the street'. Nobody is advocating *that*, and there is no reason why reforming or indeed replacing the NHS would result in it happening. Equity of access, though it should not be prioritised over outcomes to the extent that it is, should not be dispensed with altogether.

The aim of giving everyone access to healthcare, free at

the point of delivery, is perfectly noble one. The mistake is to assume this is offered *only* within the current UK National Health Service, or indeed, *any* 'National Health Service'.

There are core areas of care that everybody should receive without having to worry about money or paying the bills. That is a view shared by almost all major developed countries. After a shattering blow, such as a cancer diagnosis or a serious injury following a road traffic accident, the last thing anyone should need to worry about is money. This is where the British public have their hearts in the right place, as the supposed 'fairness' of the system is one of the reasons people proclaim their devotion to it, although we cannot discount their understandable self-interest being an additional factor.

Is the question of 'unfairness', though, not also relevant when considering the quality and waiting times for NHS care? Is it not cruel and unjust to have an elderly personal with hip pain waiting two years for an operation, or a child with severe mental health needs wait years for a diagnosis that would help with specialist educational needs, only to get his or her assessment when the damage has already been done?

Of all the boxes the NHS ticks, 'access' has always been one of the standouts, although even this is being strained to breaking point: people are spending hours on the phone just to book a GP appointment, or up to thirty hours on a trolley outside A&E. Life is unfair enough as it is, and punishing people who have become ill with disagreeable diseases or an unfortunate accident is both cruel and unnecessary.

Protecting people from exposure to catastrophic costs is one of the few elements of the NHS that does put the service in some credit, however. Even the system in Singapore, which is pretty much world renowned, has not solved this problem and people do still slip through the cracks. The lifting of *direct* financial burdens off the patient can be a good thing, although in a money hungry service, much of this is likely to be paid back over time by higher taxes as part of the cycle of dependence and redistribution.

There is also the argument that being under financial strain causes a great deal of stress, thus leading to mental health problems such as chronic anxiety, which in turn puts even *more* demand on the service. It may be better, therefore, for an agency to step in to provide help but this agency does not have to be the state. It could be a health service paid for by the state, but independent of it, or a state or private insurer, or a non-profit organisation. Just because the state is not paying directly, it does not follow that some equivalent of a Victorian workhouse would take over responsibility, still less that patients would be 'thrown onto the street'.

The philosophy of the NHS appears to be beyond domestic criticism or nuance. This attitude seems to end at the UK border however, as citizens of the developed world often look on the NHS as backward, and are nervous about relying on it if they became ill during a UK visit.

Curiously, the NHS does seem to have one specific advantage over other healthcare systems, though it is often controversial, being met with huge amounts of negative publicity. This is the overt rationing that takes place within the service, especially when it comes to treatment. NICE (the National Institute for Clinical Excellence) is the arbiter of which drugs can be approved for use on the NHS. In deciding which drugs to license, the institute leans heavily toward an evidence-led, value for money approach.

This often generates unpleasant headlines in newspapers, especially when a certain cancer drug is not licensed due to a combination of a limited survival benefit and a huge cost. But this consideration of value for money is vitally important. Though some of NICE's decisions are framed as heartless, they are the result of an honest dialogue with the public, coupled with a (surprisingly rare, by NHS standards) admission that rationing is inevitable, and that difficult decisions must be made in any system not in possession of limitless funds. We have some of the most able and dedicated medical staff in the world, those who have not already left at any rate, and it is notable that doctors usually agree with NICE recommendations, which are strictly evidence-based.

The name of the NHS is something of a misnomer. Rather than being called the 'National Health Service', which gives the misleading picture of a public health body, it should be called the NSS, or National Sickness Service.

But, rather than just *treating* the sick, it is far more important (and far cheaper) to stop people getting sick in the first place. Prevention is an incontrovertible role of healthcare, and public health campaigns are used in almost all developed countries, including the United States. In fact, promotion of good health is more important than ever in the UK, which is in the grip of an obesity epidemic, one that leads to scores of expensive to treat, preventable illnesses, such as Type 2 Diabetes. An emphasis on prevention also gives some responsibility back to the patient, who is then able to make lifestyle choices that reduce the chance of avoidable illness. This can lower the risk of sliding into dependency, a situation in which patients rely on medical staff to make clinical decisions on their behalf, or worse, end up on state handouts. All this while those who take advice to keep themselves fit and healthy end up coughing up the bill via increased taxation (another way in which the NHS is not as fair as it may first appear).

We are not North Korea, but we resemble the hermit kingdom in our fingers-in-ears mentality, convinced our 'system' is the best one. *Juche* ideology is theirs, NHS fetishisation is ours. The statues of Kim Il Sung standing outside his supposed birthplace near Mt Paektu in the North Korean Mountains bring an uncomfortable parallel with Nye Bevan's statue in Cardiff. This cherished but imperfect politician, who has approached deification not just on the left, but throughout the country has left a questionable legacy that nobody in power feels able to tamper with.

If North Korea is a state based on a delusion, then the *NHS* delusion is the nearest we get in our country.

6. PRIMARY COLOURS
General Practice

As ninety percent of all NHS consultations take place in General Practices, we should examine the daily experience of doctors and patients in them. This is primary care now in the UK, broad brushed, of course, but based on reality.

The patients' point of view first. At eight thirty in the morning, the phone lines open. Cue pandemonium. Within moments, patients are told they are number twenty (or thirty or forty) in the queue. After up to two hours of waiting on the phone, many will simply give up. Some, out of sheer frustration, some head directly to their GP surgery as a 'walk in' and demand to be seen. This may get them put on the list.

Those with some technical ability can fill out an e-consult, and this can result in a guarantee that the patient will be called back by six-thirty the following day. But the proportion of the elderly who cannot navigate the internet do not have this option, and so will leave handwritten notes in reception, which are then sent to the doctors to deal with as they see fit. As far as many elderly patients are concerned, therefore, the doctor's surgery is effectively closed.

Because there are not enough doctors, and not enough receptionists to answer the phones, getting an appointment is very difficult. The system has no utility, is faceless, and is frequently useless. High levels of dissatisfaction naturally ensue. General practitioners are pilloried in the media, accused of hiding behind the phones, being work-shy, or of using COVID as an excuse not to see patients, and so on. I have often taken calls from angry patients, who ask why it takes so long to get through on the phone, or else say things like: 'my wife had to wait for two hours', or 'why can't I get an appointment?' In summary, there are a lot of very pissed-off patients, with some degree of justification.

Now let us look at things from the GP's point of view. The e-consults, because they can be filled in ahead of time, flood your list at 8am, before you have even started. Your receptionists are stressed out because of the abuse they routinely get from patients, and high staff turnover. The latter is inevitable: at any time, reception can have three to five staff off sick with stress. 'We will not tolerate abuse' signs are put up everywhere, but admin staff are still verbally abused on a daily basis: such experiences are now, sadly, part of the job.

It is difficult for patients to wait on the phones, but those who do wait *will* get an appointment. Statistics show that forty-four percent of NHS patients who try and make an appointment on the day receive one[52]. This is unheard of in most of the developed world, even in red carpet private sectors.

Overspill normally goes to the duty or 'on call' doctor, who deals with things that cannot wait but are unsuitable for hospital admission. The duty doctor is frequently completely overwhelmed.

The BMA estimates that twenty-four patient contacts a day is safe. Numbers higher than this lead to stressed doctors and poor decision making. But in reality, it is not unknown to have over *ninety* patient contacts per day. Personally, I frequently have sixty to seventy contacts in one day. This can be a mixture of phone calls, face to face appointments, and prescheduled appointments, such as antenatal checks, baby checks, chronic disease management reviews, and home visits.

Over a decade ago, I worked briefly as a locum in a failing practice in London, where I once had seventy-three patient contacts in a single day. This was appalling and dreadful, but was, I assumed, a one off. I dined out on this anecdote for a few years. A fourteen-hour day! And yet I now expect this at least every couple of weeks. GPs are overrun. The workload never stops rising; you can rarely get on top of your admin tasks; and your days are so long and congested that you worry about killing someone. So, in summary, we have a lot of very fed-up doctors, nurses, and receptionists.

Both the client and the provider are faced with a system that *does not work*. You might say that the booking system could be changed back to the way it was 'pre-pandemic', so everyone has a face-to-face appointment as a default, and that this way, things would soon get back to normal. A nice thought, but consider that one of my locum GP practices, where I carried out some agency work, had six thousand appointment requests pre-pandemic per month, against an availability of about four thousand appointments. Once the daily emergencies were taken account of, this worked out as a two to three week wait for a GP appointment, which was typical pre-COVID.

Since the pandemic, however, the number of calls and requests for appointments had increased to *thirteen thousand* a month. We calculated that if the system was returned to a 'ring up and book in' face-to-face one, the wait for an appointment would now be eight weeks. As many ailments cannot wait that long, the system would be unworkable, and the on-call doctor would be so flooded with 'on the day' patients that disaster would ensue.

Telephone triage, deployed by some practices during the pandemic, has been retained. This system, provided you can get through on the phone, or can successfully submit an e-consult, gives the patient a decent chance of getting a same day appointment. If the patient has a problem that cannot be solved by a phone call, such as a testicular or breast lump, they will normally get a same day, face-to-face slot, followed by a rapid referral. But nobody likes this system, either, which begs the question: how bad do things have to get before people start looking at the NHS itself?

Another facet of day-to-day GP workload is the number of benefit forms that need completing. Whether filling in Universal Credit or PIP forms, this is unpaid work, and for the most part needs to be fitted around an existing clinical workload. We must ask: is this really the best use of a GP's time?

A sign-off from a doctor is sometimes inevitable in the benefit system, but some of these forms are astonishingly long. Filling in benefit forms is not something you learn how to do at medical school, and is just another way to channel the doctor into the life of a public sector drone, policing the welfare system, rather than diagnosing or treating the sick. Again, we are keeping the doctor away from what he or she does best – seeing patients.

What politicians and some members of the public simply cannot seem to understand, despite vast amounts of evidence, is that the system is *completely broken*. The demand is simply too great. Whatever GP practices do to stem the tide, it will not be enough. There is simply too much patient demand, and there are not enough appointments. Both patients and GPs are exasperated and can see there is a problem. The system is collapsing under its own weight; it is doomed.

Patient complaints often miss the point. Do they think that doctors and nursing staff are work-shy, or are trying to fob them off? Certain sections of the media have called GPs lazy, especially since the pandemic began. But the medical profession does not tend to attract lazy people. While there may be some front-line medical staff who are lazy, I have met very few of them and I suspect their number is proportionally less than most other professions. Caring professions do not tend to attract heartless bastards, either. So the question remains: are doctors and nurses *deliberately* not seeing patients? Of course not. The system, the NHS, is at fault, as it results in the link between supply and demand being severed. The resulting mismatch means we end up with a system that is not fit for purpose. More discerning sections of the media have picked up on this, but both politicians and wider public opinion still seem extremely reluctant to pin the blame on the NHS itself.

A myth has come into being, one that is fuelled by certain sections of the media: hospitals and the secondary care sector are staffed by hard-working doctors, whereas GPs idle away 'on the golf course', never answer the phone, and keep patient contact to a minimum.

If there are any lazy GPs in the NHS, I certainly have not seen any.

A recent article about a surgeon with experience of both the

NHS and private sector revealed the astonishing slowness of his working day (when working for the NHS) due to inefficiency and staff shortages[53]. He used the example of parking spaces to contrast the NHS with the private sector. As a consultant surgeon within the NHS, he was allowed access to the hospital staff car park. It was, however, small and inadequate, and was situated some distance from the hospital. Consultants who cannot access staff car parks are sometimes forced to simply park in patients' spaces, pay the fees, and then claim them back (a cumbersome process).

When working at his private hospital, the surgeon has a designated parking space near the hospital entrance. This means that he can be scrubbed up and ready in the operating theatre far more quickly. The priority is, of course, to get him operating as soon as he can, so he is able to perform as many procedures as possible.

The private sector, in which time is money, will naturally try to remove any obstacle that may get in the way of a surgeon working quickly. The NHS does not. Inbuilt inefficiency can lead to large gaps between operations, with surgeons sitting around twiddling their thumbs, waiting as patients are unhurriedly brought up to the operating theatre. Consider, too, whether you would want to be operated on by a pissed off surgeon who had just spent an hour trying to find a parking space. I know I would not.

In the UK, GPs are generally assigned about two thousand patients on their individual lists. You would expect, therefore, that a large practice of, say, sixteen thousand patients would have about eight full-time GPs. In reality, there is normally slightly more capacity than this, as nurse practitioners and paramedics can work alongside GPs to provide more capacity. This helps during periods of excessive demand, or when doctors are on leave, especially at pinch points such as school holidays. But the level of demand is unsustainable.

Many practices are in this situation, so what should they do? Trying shifting the appointments to 'e-consults'? Try to introduce telephone triage questions to stem demand? To use the out of hours service more judiciously (a service that is already under severe pressure)? Add locum staff to help with a particularly bad week, or surge of patients? But the workload keeps *coming and coming and coming*.

The consequence of doctors and nurses being overwhelmed, worked ever harder, and taking abuse for the privilege is not difficult to guess. *Burnout*, which can also lead to a lack of compassion for patients and dread of the job itself. This situation, in turn, leads to more clinical staff going off sick, thus increasing the workload for those left behind. A vicious cycle ensues. The first to go are the doctors who are a bit slower and more methodical, who do not like being hurried. The more efficient, businesslike doctors are then left to cope with the extra work. And they do cope, initially, despite their already busy days having been made busier still by having to cover for absent colleagues.

But then the situation becomes permanent: long-term sickness is converted into a resignation, thus shrinking the workforce. Eventually, even the more efficient doctor also gets burnt out and quits, until there is only a skeleton staff, which is a disaster for continuity of care. The practice then goes under, and the one or two remaining partners hand back their contract to the local health authority. The practice is then run using locums (if they can be found), or it is simply closed. In the last few years, this has been happening up and down the country. Hundreds of practices have closed and *nothing* seems to remedy the problem, not more money, not more golden hellos, not more recruitment[54]. It does not matter how much money they pay you to do an impossible job: the job will still be impossible.

Imagine for a moment this situation taking place in the private sector, or in a mixed system. Supply and demand mean that market forces would be at work. In the NHS, if a GP sees one or one hundred patients a day, they will be paid the same. But think of all that demand. A private or NHS clinic would have no difficulty whatsoever recruiting if doctors were paid per patient. One hundred patients will earn the doctor, if not an exact multiple, certainly a damn sight more than seeing *one* patient, unless that patient is Elon Musk, or the Sultan of Brunei. Recruitment would not be difficult. A busy clinic with loads of patients *should* be expanding all the time, in the same way that a busy restaurant should, rather than turning diners away, increase its number of tables.

The socialists would doubtless object to the idea of introducing payments per patient into the system, as it would be 'against the founding principles of the NHS'. But, as I will come to later, plenty of health services around the world pay their doctors and nurses by workload and performance, even in direct billing systems. The assumption that matching supply to demand leads irrevocably to out-of-pocket payments or inequality of access is a false one.

As it stands, NHS recruitment is a complete disaster. Who on earth would want to go through years of study, only to be overworked, underappreciated, underpaid, and, sometimes, verbally abused? All these factors are magnified when trying to recruit practices nurses, health care assistants, and receptionists, who are paid less money and get even more abuse.

All this has led many doctors and nurses to emigrate in search of a better life abroad. In the UK, there is an annual exodus of clinicians, and almost all of them cite the pressure, stress, and misery of working in the NHS as their reason for leaving. (Pay is, interestingly, mentioned much less often than other factors). I have had many colleagues, including paramedics, nurses, doctors, physiotherapists, and highly trained ITU specialist nurses, who have left with no intention of coming back. This phenomenon has created a recruitment crisis.

The NHS will likely fill the gaps with increased training places, but this will take a long time, and if it not done alongside a true reform of the system, many of these newcomers will also go part-time or leave.

Traditionally, gaps in the service have often been filled by immigrants. Indeed, the NHS has a huge percentage of immigrants in its workforce already, and would collapse without them. This is often cited by proponents of mass immigration as a reason to open our borders to more health workers from abroad. While many of the immigrants who work in the NHS do excellent work, their presence is a reflection of the failure of our own country to train (and retain) our own staff. We are therefore forced to recruit doctors from far poorer countries, countries where they may, in fact, be desperately needed. If the NHS would collapse without immigrants, it does not say much for the NHS.

Do the public really love their NHS? The statistics prove otherwise. Over a twelve-month period, between 2016 and 2017, there were over fifty-six thousand physical assaults on NHS staff[55], a figure that has since risen dramatically year on year. Consider the fact that this figure does not include verbal abuse: if it did, the figures would be much higher. Consider, too, that this figure comes from England alone.

This amounts to over two hundred assaults per day, and these are only the *reported* incidents. I have known friends and colleagues fail to report violent assaults, as they have become so routine. We must ask what causes the public to behave in this way. Overly high expectations? A sense of entitlement? A lack of respect? It could be all these things.

In the past few years, the job of a GP has changed beyond all recognition. Previously, GPs were able to book many of their patients as follow ups, for the management of long-term medical conditions. But the job has now become so busy that everything is crisis management.

Patients no longer ring up depressed, they ring up because they are suicidal. When you get to the third or fourth suicidal patient of the day, this transference on to your own personality is horribly draining, leaving many doctors only just above the burnout waterline. There is no special training, no debrief, no pastoral care. You suck it up and take it home with you. Well, some of us can. I worry about those that cannot. Any when you look again you find out they have buggered off to Australia. And who can blame them?

A newly diagnosed type 2 diabetic will turn up already having have appalling blood sugar control (an emergency situation), compared with a marginally raised reading that will subsequently need to be controlled as the disease progresses. At all times, the job is effectively on an emergency footing. But this is primary care, not Accident and Emergency. Crisis management is not what GPs trained for.

Some older patients frequently make complaints such as: 'oh, you are my alleged doctors are you', 'Dr Smith is my doctor but I have only even seen him twice', or 'I do not even bloody know who my doctor is'. What I think they are trying to say is: 'in my day, doctors knew all their patients, made home visits at the drop of a hat, were on personal terms with all the patients and their families, delivered babies, gave out handwritten scribbled prescriptions, and worked all hours'.

This may indeed have been the case fifty years ago, but since I started, this sepia-tinted view of the family doctor (and the hospital consultant) has been made an impossibility. Even if doctors wanted to live up to these sky-high expectations, there is no way they would be able to deliver them. This is not to say that patients do not need or deserve home visits, or to see the same doctor each time. It is to say that such a service is logistically impossible in today's climate.

Since GPs opted out of providing round the clock care, there has been much hand wringing and grumbling, some stating that the provision of round the clock care is an integral part of the role of the GP (or practice), and that it should not be outsourced to an out of hours co-operative. Yet in most of the healthcare systems I have examined, and certainly in the countries I have worked in, this is not the case. In Singapore and Australia, there was no home visiting, and the option was not even mentioned, as both systems had established out of hours services. And, given the intensity of UK general practice today,

I cannot imagine anyone would be happy with a knackered GP getting up in the middle of the night to come and see them, even if they have consulted with the same clinician a couple of times at the practice before.

A colleague of mine, at his previous practice, once asked his PPG (patient participation group) to come up with what they wanted from the surgery, because the number of complaints was so great (the complaints were about process, not medical errors). The same thing kept coming back: 'I want to see the doctor of my choice, seven days a week, at a time of my convenience'. Great, if you are looking for a private GP in Chelsea, although I know private GPs in Chelsea, and I am not sure even they would be able to meet this level of expectation. Such demands are not rooted in any sort of reality: they are simply impossible to satisfy with a state-run, taxpayer funded service like the NHS. The media and politicians also do not help, pumping out propaganda that the NHS is the envy of the world, thus raising the public's expectations to ludicrous levels. Much discord and dissatisfaction regarding the NHS comes from these expectations, and the bigger the gap between the expectation and reality, the more fed up the patient becomes. This is true in both the NHS and the private sector, and can apply to expectations and attitudes to antibiotics, waiting times and so on.

Younger patients are trained in dependence, and some view the NHS security blanket with a sense of entitlement. I know of one patient in her early thirties who had a minor hospital procedure to drain an abscess, and was asked to follow up with her own GP to arrange dressings on alternate days for two weeks. After her first appointment with our practice nurse, she asked if the rest of her appointments could take place at home, as she was having to rely on her boyfriend to drive her to the surgery, and Ubers were too expensive. This patient was not housebound and, other than her recent minor issue, was in perfect health.

An appointment at the surgery is relatively quick and inexpensive for the taxpayer. A district nurse visit, however, costs an awful lot more money. I know what the district nurse list was like on the day the patient made her request. They had a full workload, and were, naturally, understaffed. Their list included an elderly lady with dementia who needed a bladder and bowel assessment due to her faecal incontinence, a very elderly gentlemen who was bedbound and struggling with his catheter, and an end-of-life patient who needed a syringe driver set up to administer morphine for terminal cancer.

But the young patient, without any self-reflection or insight, requested a home visit. I cannot record the district nurses' reply to this request, but it was approximate to '*go forth and procreate*'. It was then left to me to explain to the patient that the request was inappropriate, but she still, astonishingly, struggled to understand quite *why* it was inappropriate.

This episode demonstrates not only the utter disconnect between patients' idea of what is possible, and what can actually be provided on the NHS, it also shows a lack of moral clarity regarding what *should* be available on the NHS. It must be understood that, if the service is not used responsibly, it collapses. There used to be an unwritten and unspoken contact between NHS staff and patients to use the service according to their needs, rather than their wants. Not anymore.

Medical professionals have traditionally been the recipients of a large amount of respect and even deference from the British people. Now. I cannot speak for hospital consultants, but as far as GPs go, respect is a dead as Harold Shipman. It is difficult to trace exactly when the decline in the status of doctors started, or what reasons lie behind it. Again, to use GPs as an example, it may be because an increased workload has led to much less time with each patient. Another theory is that if a service is 'free' and you are entitled to it, you lose respect for it, as it is stripped of all sense of rarity and privilege. It is interesting to contrast the situation in the UK with the one in countries that do not have single-payer systems, such as the USA or Israel, where doctors are far more venerated.

Whatever the reason, this loss of respect is very real, and pervades many aspects of the average GP's day.

Now that we have discussed the side of the job that is visible to the public, the telephone calls and face-to-face appointments, we come to the unseen fatberg in the sewer of the GP's working day: the administrative side of the job. Just as frustrating as a fatberg, but unlike the latter, which, as an accumulation of non-perishable waste, can be broken down with a high-pressure hose, a GP's admin is self-perpetuating: no matter how much of a dent you make in it, however early you come to work, or however late you stay in the evenings, it is always there. Not so much the elephant in the room as the huge woolly mammoth, the one that has just broken free from its icy hibernation and taken a Stone Age dump next to the skirting board.

Administration takes many forms in primary care, but the core areas are: prescriptions, hospital letters, test results, and a whole host of other random tasks. Such tasks can involve a combination of the other three, but do not require actual patient contact. An example of this would be renewing a sick note.

During my registrar year, almost twenty years ago, you were on a rota for your daily duty. If you were on prescriptions, the practice nurse would give you a foolscap folder of scripts to sign. This would, if you were unlucky, take twenty minutes. If you were on 'labs', your task was a simple actioning of results for the practice. Extracting dates from hospital letters would take a similar amount of time. And that would be the admin for the day. The only miscellaneous rota item was the home visit. If this was your allocated task, you were on visits for the whole practice. The number of visits could range from zero to three and, although the visits could be time-consuming, you would have plenty of space in your day to carry them out.

Contrast that with the present situation, especially post-pandemic. We GPs have our own list of patients, and rather than going by rotas, must carry out most of the home visits ourselves, do all our own scripts, action all the lab results, and read and act on all the hospital documents.

In summary, there is now more administration for each individual GP than there was for an *entire practice* two decades ago. The simple foolscap folder has long since gone, and our (now computerised) inboxes bulge with over one hundred scripts per day, all of which need to be electronically signed; fifty or sixty lab results that must be painstakingly gone through; endless documents to act upon; and an ever-lengthening list of other tasks. This can take up to three hours, or, if you are covering for someone, even longer.

So what, you may say – surely admin is simply part of

the job? This is true, but there are two points to be made. Firstly, that the amount of administration has gotten out of control in the last fifteen years, especially over the last five years. And secondly, that this level of admin, when compared to the amount done in a day by a GP in the private sector, is overwhelming. Private GPs spend over ninety percent of their working day with patients, using their brains for patient interactions and diagnostics, rather than mundane tasks.

The inefficiency of the NHS system, coupled with the lack of any admin filter, means that GPs can easily spend forty percent of their days on admin alone. It is rather like the cliche of the policeman who spends hours each day on an old-fashioned typewriter, filling out paperwork, rather than wandering the streets and catching criminals.

Which would you prefer: a doctor up to their ears in paperwork, or a doctor with a streamlined administrative workload who has far more time to listen to you? I know GPs who have left their jobs purely because of the huge amount of admin, preferring to locum instead (a role that is better paid, and involves less admin).

Another huge problem is that of *duplication*, which has a direct bearing on admin. A colleague told me about an example of this recently: a patient with known osteoarthritis was referred to the musculoskeletal team (at which first point of contact the patient can then be transferred to a physiotherapist, a rheumatologist, an orthopaedic surgeon, and so on). The team diagnosed adhesive capsulitis, or frozen shoulder, which can be difficult to treat with physiotherapy or painkillers. The patient was referred for an ultrasound-guided joint injection, which can be performed by an interventional radiologist or an orthopaedic doctor. The wait for the appointment was several months, by which time identical symptoms had arisen in the opposite arm. Yet at the appointment, rather than injecting both shoulders, which would not have taken very long at all, the patient was advised to go back to his GP to request a second referral for the other shoulder. More pointless wasted appointments, and another large time delay. How ridiculous, you may think. The patient certainly did, as he then gave up and went private to get his second injection, paying for it himself. His insurance would not cover it, as his previous referral showed this was a 'pre-existing condition'. Sadly, this sort of nonsense happens on a regular basis, much to the frustration and annoyance of everyone involved.

This story is only a small example of the waste of time and effort that is caused by primary care doctors not having open access to testing, due to the misguided rationing of MRI scanner services. A GP with access to an MRI could get a firm diagnosis much more rapidly, and would then be able to send the patient to the end point service that is needed. This would save a huge amount of time and money. But the problem is not *just* the rationing, it is that there are not enough MRI scanners to begin with. Indeed, the lack of rapid access, high technology diagnostic equipment and those trained in its use is a colossal failure for the NHS, leading to delays in the detection and treatment of diseases from cancer to multiple sclerosis[56].

This is *exactly* the area in which a more results and outcome focused management would invest heavily, allocating the correct resources and training to the sharp end, where they are really needed. Alas, this is not the priority of the NHS. Equity is everything. If you ended up with more MRI scanners in London per person than a deprived area of the north, the 'founding principles of the NHS' would be violated. So we continue to stumble on with the same top down, piss-poor services.

It is even more of a pity when you consider that British trained GPs are the best in the world, certainly the best of any country I have worked in. The sheer volume of work they do, while exhausting, gives them a level of all-round clinical experience and expertise that is unmatched. It is therefore heartbreaking to see so many move abroad and never come back, thus forcing the NHS to recruit from other countries, whose graduates may be decent doctors, but have not grown up 'in the system' and so cannot navigate it for patients in the same way, or communicate as efficiently and effectively as our home-trained staff, due to the inevitable cultural differences.

Since the origin of the NHS, most GP practices have been run on a partnership model. Before then, GPs were effectively running their own small businesses, often practising single handedly and with little oversight. After the health service was nationalised, they carried on as before, but now had a single customer: the NHS. Partners remained self-employed, continuing to run their practices as businesses, albeit ones that were ever more strictly regimented. Doctors themselves employed the staff, such as the receptionists and practice nurses, and were responsible for funding all expenses of the practice from an overall lump sum. GPs could also see private patients on the side, but were only allowed to earn a certain percentage of their income this way.

GPs made their pact with the new service but, even within the nominal autonomy of partnership, they lost independence and status, being seen first by the government and then by the general public as mere public sector employees. Earnings were also eroded over time. In the fifties, GPs such as Hugh Laurie's father could afford to send their children to Eton. In the eighties, the family doctor in our village in West Oxfordshire could send his only child to Radley. But in the present day, such instances are a rarity.

Fiscal drift has resulted in GPs having large chunks of their earning swallowed up by higher tax brackets. Added to this are daft pension rules that result in large numbers of GPs working part time or retiring early, as it is not cost effective to do otherwise. It is difficult to imagine what a standard full time GP would earn if exposed to the full pressure of market forces. The true answer I suppose is that it depends on the GP.

With government control comes increased regulation and ever more complex and onerous appraisals, assessments and 'revalidations', along with a target driven culture swallowing up huge amounts of time that could otherwise be spent with patients. This leads to ever more boredom, disillusionment, and low morale.

Partly as a result, the last few decades have seen the emergence of the 'salaried' GP, a doctor employed directly by, and therefore the responsibility of, the practice. Being employed as a salaried GP usually results in having a lower income than a partner, but it brings with it all the advantages of being an employee, such as paid holiday, maternity, and sick leave. You can also lose your job, of course, although given the chronic GP shortage you will find work again soon enough. I have colleagues who are very happily salaried, although they do tend to be part-time. The best practices are run for the benefit of all the doctors (those who are partners, and those who are salaried), all the ancillary staff, and all the patients.

Since the introduction of salaried GPs, governments of both political stripes have fought to freeze NHS pay. This has resulted in a drift down of income in real terms, suppressing partnership earnings and therefore narrowing the gap between the incomes of partner and salaried GPs. Partnerships jobs, especially full-time partnerships, are much less desirable, and tend to have few applicants. Salaried jobs should, therefore, be more attractive, sacrificing a small amount of pay for much better working conditions and less admin. But in reality, advertisements for salaried jobs also receive very few applicants, and are sometimes impossible to fill. GPs have not vanished, but we now have such a chronic shortage that large numbers of GPs (including some partners) have opted to become self-employed locums. With an endless supply of work in a sellers' market, locums can charge high rates and take holidays whenever they want. The advantages outweigh the lack of continuity, stability, and status. The number of locums has grown exponentially, and is costing the NHS a fortune. The same issue is also affecting secondary care in hospitals, especially in A&E, although secondary care doctors are more likely to be carrying out extra duties in addition to their regular jobs, rather than being a full-time locums.

Primary Care in the NHS is not in a good state. Demand, fuelled by high expectations, is increasing at a rapid rate, while the supply of GPs has shuddered to a halt and the remaining workforce has started to shrink. Practices are moving mountains to deliver record numbers of appointments, which politicians are happy to take credit for, while the government frequently comes up with new wheezes to appease patients struggling to get an appointment. This results in yet more targets, and in more work for GPs, without any extra funding.

Understandably fed-up patients, burnt out doctors, and harassed practice staff: in short, a completely broken primary care sector. Anyone who thinks this is a fit state for a first world service is labouring under a delusion.

7. OUT OF SIGHT...
Mental Health

Attitudes to mental health have changed enormously over the last two or three decades, both inside and outside the medical profession. Sadness has been medicalised to a far greater extent than before, and the number of diagnosed cases of conditions that have more recently entered the public consciousness, such as attention deficit hyperactivity disorder (ADHD), has soared.

Is this a good thing? It is rather difficult to say. The road to hell is paved with good intentions, and medicalising day-to-day emotions can lead to seriously unexpected consequences. Sadness is endemic to the human condition: there is no evidence that sadness is any more an abnormal emotion than happiness is, for example. Most animals live in a state of fear or predation or starvation, often all three, and the occasional period of contentment is all they can hope for. This may sound trite, but it is important, as the public increasingly view happiness as some sort of norm, and sadness as an illness that ought to be treated by the medical profession.

An overall commentary on recent events in psychiatry, and the extent to which they are applicable to the wider populace, is outside the brief of this book. Our concern lies with the way that changing attitudes and expectations in this area affect the

NHS, and with the extra healthcare burden that must then be shouldered. We have already explored the founding of the NHS, including Beveridge's ideas about personal responsibility, and the contributory principle, noting that these aspects of the NHS's original premise have vanished from the debate in the UK. Questions such as: 'do I really need to speak to the doctor about this', or: 'can I manage on my own' are asked by fewer and fewer people.

The workload that mental health problems generate is of serious concern in a single-payer government-funded system, as mental health places huge demands on healthcare staff and resources. It is also relevant that most management of mental health conditions does not deal in cures. Many afflictions are ill-defined, difficult to treat, and lifelong. In addition, there is the economic burden caused by millions of sick days due to depression alone[57]. The effect on staff can also be exhausting and demoralising. Not only can people present with intractable problems involving a huge social component, but there is the added lack of job satisfaction that comes with conditions a health professional can only manage, at best, rather than cure. If you are a trained counsellor or psychologist working for the NHS, with thirty-minute appointments, this goes with the territory, but for rushed GPs, or Acute Mental Health Teams (AMHTs), dealing with such misery can be soul-destroying.

Mental health problems are complex. They are often multi-factorial, and take time and investment to deal with. For desperate patients and overstretched doctors, it is all too easy to go for a quick fix, reaching for anti-depressants, for example, rather than joining a long waiting list for counselling. When huge numbers of the population in some parts of the UK end up on these drugs, the diagnosis itself becomes almost meaningless, as the prevalence of the condition informs us that we are dealing with a variant of normality[58]. It is very unlikely that twenty-eight percent of the public are suffering from moderate to severe depression, which is the only type, as opposed to milder forms of the condition, with a good evidence base for pharmaceutical treatment. For milder symptoms, counselling is recommended. This often comes in the form of CBT, which has a better evidence base for mild depression than pharmaceutical treatment, although it is still not as good as one might assume[59].

Expectations of instant cures can also lead to a complete lack of self-reliance. In a 'free' system such as the NHS, which has abandoned its contributory principle, this can all too often manifest as an unhealthy sense of entitlement and dependence.

A colleague of mine was called by a young female patient whose two-year-old was playing up and would not go to sleep. This had been going on for over a week. It is true that this sort of thing can, sometimes, be a cry for help from a non-coping parent who is under psychological duress in some way. But it is often, as in this case, more of a 'can't be bothered' situation: the mother proceeded to ask for medication (melatonin) to help the child sleep. Fine, if this was a one-off, and fine too if a calm explanation that this was *not* a justification for a doctor's appointment would suffice: the parent, now suitably educated, could be empowered to deal with this problem by herself in future. But no, at the merest suggestion that this was not a life-threatening issue the mother went berserk, resulting in a formal complaint being made to the practice.

I have had similar consultations with adults, whose

presenting complaint is simply: 'I cannot get to sleep'. But once it has been established that there is no underlying primary diagnosis of anxiety, it is not always clear where the 'medicine' is here, either. Most people have spells when they find sleep a struggle. Occasionally, it can be debilitating, and a small number of sleeping tablets may help in the short term. But I seriously doubt that, in the eighties and nineties, we had anything like the current volume of patients turning up at their GP complaining that they 'can't get to sleep'.

Another example concerns a patient who called the surgery in tears saying that she had just been sacked, was driving home, and could be at the doctor's surgery in thirty minutes. Being sacked is very unpleasant, and surely not one of life's best experiences, but, unfortunate as it may be, is just not really a medical problem. What next, you drop a bag of shopping, break all your eggs, and proceed to call the doctors in tears?

Sadly, NHS ambulances have been called for less. One wonders just what flashes through the patient's mind – I have just been sacked, do I ring my boss's secretary to ask them to reconsider, or arrange another meeting? Do I speak to my best friend? Do I call one of my colleagues? Or do I ring a family member, for guaranteed tea and sympathy? No, I'll call the *GP*. Where did all this start?

We are not talking about someone who has lost their job, whose personal hygiene has gone, who no longer leaves the house to socialise, and, after several weeks, has dropped weight as they have lost interest in eating. These would be signs of severe depression, and the loss of job, although easily identifiable as the trigger, would become incidental to the diagnosis. No, we are taking about having a bad day and calling the doctor. Not all cases are this extreme, but most NHS GPs will be able to recall a case like this, following which, after they have put the phone down, or the door has closed, they think: 'What has this go to do with me? I did not train for this'. GPs are primary healthcare professionals, not lifestyle coaches.

The issue with this sort of complaint, and many other social problems that can end up on a GP's list, is that they are more time consuming than most physical problems, and difficult to conclude. There is the problem of 'transference', which entails personal trauma being redirected to a substitute, often a healthcare professional. This redirection of the initial symptom causes the professional to soak up the misery of the patient like a sponge. Psychologists with specialist training may be able to keep a cool professional distance and block out such feelings, but most GPs and first line providers end up with a ruined day at best and clinical exhaustion and burnout at worst.

As the legend has it, St. Christopher carried the infant Jesus across a river thinking it would be easy, but, halfway across, the child grew as heavy as the sorrows of the whole world. NHS staff cannot be a legion of St. Christophers. There are not enough psychiatrists for this, or trained counsellors, let alone GPs. The explosion in the medicalisation of low mood has clogged appointment lists to the extent that those who really do need help, those with severe clinical depression, chronic anxiety, or post-traumatic stress, have their voices drowned out by the cacophony, of me, me, me, from essentially healthy individuals. If there were plenty of appointments to go round, that would be one thing. But, if there is one area where critics of recent Conservative governments have a point regarding underfunding, then it is surely that of mental health services, which have been starved to beggary.

The most recent addition to the mental health high table of arbitrary diagnoses is the much-misunderstood developmental disorder, first known as the 'hyperkinetic reaction of childhood', then as Attention Deficit Disorder (ADD), and now as Attention Deficit Hyperactivity Disorder (ADHD).

This condition, or set of symptoms, was initially formalised in the USA in 1987[60]. The numbers diagnosed with it have increased year on year, as have the resultant prescriptions of amphetamine related medications such as methylphenidate. Seven percent of children qualify for a diagnosis, with boys being affected far more than girls. Guidelines in the United States appear to recommend intervention with medication at an earlier stage compared to the UK, where there is, mercifully, more resistance to the practice of giving very young children strong medications that have associated side effects. Some states in the US have a diagnosis rate of over thirteen percent, an extraordinary figure[61].

Whilst ADHD certainly does seem to exist, and most doctors support its classification as a developmental disorder, opinion is not unanimous. To speak of my own experience, I have referred primary school age children who literally cannot sit still: they destroy my consulting room, ripping up the paper on the examination couch, opening all the cupboards and drawers, and grabbing at expensive medical equipment. Such behaviours are not 'normal', and it would seem appropriate to refer such children for a complete assessment and (possible) diagnosis.

When practicing abroad, I saw whole families, especially

American and Canadian ones, in which both parents and all the children had not only been diagnosed with ADHD, but were also all on the same medication, albeit at different doses. I have known of American students who take their methylphenidate for a few days at exam time to 'help them concentrate'. This is ridiculous: the medication is not intended to be used in this way, and should always be prescribed in conjunction with regular psychological evaluation and monitoring.

What seems to be a new phenomenon, one that I have only noticed since returning to the UK, is the number of patients on the NHS who are now seeking this diagnosis. Whilst the number of children who have been diagnosed with ADHD is rather worrying (although compared to my practice abroad, relatively few seem to be on medication), what is truly surprising is the number of adults that come forward, demanding a referral and diagnosis, and, in some cases, medication, as a *first resort*, because their children have been diagnosed and they 'recognise the same symptoms in themselves'.

The NHS is not particularly flexible at the best of times, and a large volume of referrals (it is very difficult to decline a referral, especially in the field of mental health) can easily overwhelm the system. For adults, the waiting time for an ADHD assessment can be up to two and a half years.

The huge rise in diagnosis of children with ADHD and ASD (Autism Spectrum Disorder) has societal consequences beyond medicine. The number of children now on disability benefits in the UK has jumped by over 100,000 in the last twenty years, following a surge in ADHD and ASD diagnoses[62]. In 2022, the parents of 190.000 9–13 year olds claimed disability, meaning that, incredibly, 1 in 14 children in this age group is now in receipt of the associated benefits. While the intention behind the provision of these benefits may be well meaning, one cannot help wonder if the over-medicalisation and associated stigma will lead to a life of low expectation and lack of achievement in this group, coupled with a welfare dependency that lasts into adulthood.

When adult patients call in and list their ADHD symptoms, it is instructive to ask what they hope to gain by a diagnosis. Are they so debilitated that they cannot function? Almost never. Are they gainfully employed? Can they keep a job down? What do they want to achieve? How will a diagnosis change their life? Are they aware that medication has side effects? We have questionnaires that enable us to ask the patient, and a close relative, for all the relevant information regarding their symptoms. This is required before any referral is made. Yet even when patients fall short of the diagnostic criteria, they often still insist on being given a referral.

This illustrates two problems. The first is that patients are actively seeking an ill-defined 'diagnosis' and hoping to be medicalised for it, perhaps to explain away their failures, or give them an excuse not to take responsibility for their actions. (This, surely, is a debate for sociologists or psychologists). The second is that, by insisting on referrals, such people never consider the impact on the resources of the NHS. Do they never stop and wonder *why* the waiting lists are so long? Do they consider the possibility that they may be pushing someone with more serious symptoms, who has suffered in silence for years, further down the waiting list? Could it be that there are more deserving cases out there than their own?

But therapy, counselling, and medication are not the

panaceas that many patients imagine them to be. The goal of managing mental health problems, rather than curing them, is the key, with cycles of relapse and remission being all but inevitable. The insatiable belief in happiness as a *right* is a dangerous one, and it is beyond the gift of the medical profession to make people happy.

The US Declaration of Independence promised the right to: 'Life, Liberty, and the Pursuit of Happiness'. Note that crucial word: the *pursuit*. We are all entitled to seek happiness, but it is not a given. If a person's happiness is achievable only through medication and counselling, it is not a particularly worthwhile form of happiness anyway.

It is something of a cliché to suggest that many of the great artists and thinkers of the past would, to a certain extent, be 'on the spectrum' by today's standards. Does psychiatry, by picking a particular cultural or behavioural standard as a defining point of 'normal' (which must surely be arbitrary and subjective), work against the natural diversity and richness that flows from the human condition? Are we to medicate away future painters, playwrights, comedians, or science and technology obsessives, ending up with classroom after classroom of reasonably well-behaved dullards who simply go through the motions? By medicalising emotions, do we not standardise and 'control' the personalities of the young, turning them into something that adults, whether parents, doctors or (God help us) politicians, have deemed acceptable? To use a rather overused adjective, is this not somewhat Orwellian?

One could invent any number of 'psychiatric conditions' with arbitrary diagnoses. Think of students getting stressed when sitting exams, with symptoms including nausea, flushing, sweating and insomnia. This phenomenon could be categorised as an illness. But, in reality, the 'condition' fits on a spectrum. It is merely a natural response to external stimuli that some may struggle with more than others.

The suspicion remains that the 'pill for every ill' approach, or the intensive therapy session, and the doling out of a diagnosis, is something of a short cut. We should be wary of 'quick' or 'easy' answers in psychiatry, given the complexity of our consciousness, emotional regulation, and perceptions. The proper management of mental health takes time, effort, and careful husbandry. Outcomes may be mixed, but prescribing medication to someone with deep-rooted personal issues does not take away the underlying problem, which remains unsolved, and will only re-assert itself once you take the medication away. Sadly, mental health and psychiatry often require resources the NHS simply does not have. By trying to do too much, the NHS spreads itself too thin, and only ends up doing too little, or at least not doing things properly. Mental health is not 'sexy', and ends up at the back of the queue. The cacophony of the sheer volume of people who are fed up and miserable inevitably drowns out those in the population who have severe and punishing clinical depression, or other mental health disorders, who then end up in huge queues for treatment, sometimes slipping through the net completely and taking their own lives.

This is an area in which the public could make a difference: if there was only more education about these matters, the public would have a better awareness of what psychiatry and mental health provision really is, and what its limits are. Setting realistic expectations of health care professionals and treatments would be a good place to start. By encouraging more resilience or self-help for those who are neither helpless nor alone, demand could be reduced. This also applies to 'going off sick' with mild depression or a low mood, a change that is almost guaranteed to make things worse, given that it entails the patient merely sitting at home, unoccupied. Bertrand Russell's excellent book *The Conquest of Happiness,* which is well worth a read, explores the link between boredom and misery in depth .

Mental Health services in the NHS are often not fit for purpose. You may be seen and assessed promptly if you are in the midst of crisis, but that is all the service is able to provide: crisis management. Prevention and early intervention have long since disappeared under the weight of huge demand, leading to waiting lists long enough to cause a mental health crisis by themselves. A two to three year wait even for an initial assessment is surely very poor, by anybody's standard. The result is that we no longer see patients in primary care presenting with the first signs of depression. Instead, they come to us already in crisis, often suicidal.

The explosion of mental health problems in children and young people has been a visible and tragic consequence of the government's ill-thought through lockdown policy, and has led to crippling delays in the children's mental health system. This is all the more worrying because, in that part of the system, early intervention is key in the prevention of lifelong problems. Teenagers or young adults, are often unprepared for a life that will inevitably have its failures and disappointments, be they romantic, financial, or academic. Yet rather than experience a period of introspection or self-examination, they would rather go on anti-depressants. But anti-depressants only work for those who only have moderate to severe depression, and do not help much if a person is simply pissed off, or fed up. GPs then end up increasing the dose until such patients become zombified and unfeeling. What needs to be understood is that we must all, sometimes, feel emotional pain, and not attempt to blunt it, because once you cannot feel pain, you cannot really feel *anything*.

At the beginning of the book, we defined exactly what a delusion is. It is a well-known symptom in psychiatry. Here, we have an excellent example: to expect the current supply of mental health professionals and appointments in the NHS to meet the phenomenally complex demands of mental health right across the spectrum is a delusion of the highest order.

PART TWO: THE REST

"'Monsieur is going to leave home?"
"Yes," returned Phileas Fogg. "We are going round the world.'"

- Jules Verne, Around the World in 80 Days

'True wisdom comes to each of us when we realize how little we understand about life, ourselves, and the world around us.'

- Socrates

8. SINGAPORE
The city in a garden

For hundreds of years, 'Singapura' meant a small collection of Malay fishing villages under the control of the Sultanate of Johor.

Then, in 1819, history began to catch up with the island. The first of a long line of enterprising, ambitious, hungry, and influential men arrived. These men began to steer the island in the direction of a modernity and prosperity that could once have scarcely been imagined. Sir Stamford Raffles, the acknowledged founder of Singapore, came ashore at the retrospectively designated 'landing site' in Boat Quay, where his statue stands today. It was he who transferred ownership of the island to the British East India Company.

Aided greatly by its strategic location and its free port status, Singapore sucked in migrants from the wider region, creating a unique ethnic mix of Europeans, Chinese, Indians, and Malay. The layout of the town was planned carefully by Raffles, and was divided into ethnic enclaves, such as Chinatown, Little India, and Arab Street. The Europeans, who found the climate intolerable, were soon outnumbered by the Chinese, and a melting pot of cultures emerged years before the same could be said of New York.

During the Second World War, Singapore's strategic

importance as Britain's 'Gibraltar of the East' proved all too tempting to the aggressively militaristic Japanese Empire. The Japanese invaded downwards, from the Malay peninsula (a fact which proved unfortunate for the defenders, as all Singapore's big guns faced south, the direction from which the invasion was expected to come). The subsequent surrender of Allied Forces to the Japanese troops, who were fewer in number, was the biggest disaster in British military history. British, Australian and Dutch troops went into captivity under a regime that did not treat surrender as an instrument deserving of respect. Many suffered in brutal conditions, and were never seen again.

Atom bombs and imperial overstretch were to condemn the Japanese to defeat in 1945. The Brits then returned, and Singapore was parcelled out into a 'Crown Colony' on its own. Keen to divest themselves of imperial possessions in South East Asia, the British withdrew from Singapore in 1963, although they did keep use of the large naval base until 1971.

In the interim period between the war and full independence, Singapore was permitted a large degree of self-government. Rising to become Prime Minister in 1959 was a fifth-generation Straits Chinese, a Cambridge graduate called Lee Kwan Yew. His People's Action Party (PAP) became the dominant party of government, benefiting from the approval of the West as a counterbalance to the communists and assorted leftist regional movements.

In 1963, Singapore joined Malaya in the union known as Malaysia. It was a short-lived arrangement. Due to fears of Chinese domination, partly driven by worries over the highly formidable Mr. Lee himself, Singapore was kicked out and left to become a city state on its own. With grim resolve, Mr. Lee announced the split, rolled up his shirt sleeves, and got to work.

With his emphasis on patriotism, hard work, and self-reliance, coupled with a limited welfare state, it was no coincidence Margaret Thatcher became a friend and ideological soulmate to Mr. Lee.

He did have a less attractive side, however. His will to dominate and hypersensitivity ended the career of any domestic politician or journalist who dared cross him. During a Chinese state visit to Singapore in 1978, he told Deng Xiaoping that although the Chinese were not necessarily wedded to communism, they were traditionally comfortable in an authoritarian framework[63]. Deng took his memories of the achievement of Singapore, the gleaming tower blocks and first world infrastructure, back to China with him. Soon the concept of one country, two systems, was born, and Lee's brand of authoritarian capitalism became a key factor in the rise of the Chinese superpower that now dominates the Far East.

Whatever his methods, Mr. Lee laid the ground work for an economic miracle that lives on today. The financial district, the air-conditioned mass transit system, some of the best hotels in Asia, and a highly liveable city are testament to his achievements.

For the expatriate, Singapore provides a huge number of clean, modern high-rise condominiums with pools, gyms, and BBQ pits. Wealthy residents tend to cling to the smarter downtown areas of Orchard Road and Holland Village, while the majority of locals live further out in HDB (Housing and Development Board) high rise apartments. The latter are largely reserved for citizens, and are much more affordable.

Singapore's status as a leading world financial centre makes it a destination for high earning expatriates and their families. They will, from time to time, need medical care. To cater for this community, the high-end 'Expatriate Medical Clinic' (EMC) was founded, offering GP and paediatric services. This is where I gained the job opportunity enabling me to move to Singapore.

I had a small accommodation allowance that covered about two thirds of my rent, and cheap private healthcare insurance, but I was astonished by the deals and packages enjoyed by many of my patients. Thanks to these expats, our medical clinic was never short of patients. In the decade following the 2008 world financial crisis, large companies became reluctant to offer lucrative packages to any but their top executives, preferring to hire locals. But fortunately, as our clinic had a good reputation, we were able to hold on to a good percentage of patients, even once they were downgraded to local packages.

Singapore has four official languages, English, Mandarin, Tamil, and Malay. Fortunately, English is the most widely spoken language, meaning that there were no issues with extra language requirements. The expatriate clinic's clientele could be divided into quarters: one was American, another British, and another Australian, with the final quarter being formed of a mix of nationalities. Ninety-eight percent of our patients were expatriates. The local Singaporeans would go to polyclinics (very cheap and run by the government) or local GP surgeries (more expensive, but still cheaper than our clinic).

Our clinic was in the Tanglin area, at the heart of the expatriate community and within walking distance of Orchard

Road. On my first day, I was shown to my new consulting room on the eighteenth floor. It had a spectacular view of the Chinese embassy and the immaculate buildings of the Tanglin district, all of which nestled amongst palm trees, tropical foliage, and the ubiquitous swimming pools.

The building we occupied was purpose-built as a top end out-patient medical centre. One floor was used by eye surgeons, another by dentists, another by physiotherapists, and so on. We were unique in being the only general practice in the building. Our clinic had a spacious reception area and a children's playroom. The waiting area was far more impressive than most NHS GP surgeries I had worked for. The clinic itself consisted of eight consulting rooms and four treatment rooms, used for isolation, procedures, and injections.

As is usual in Singapore, the clinic was air conditioned. The aircon started at around eight fifteen in the morning, so if you were on an 'early' shift, starting at eight, you would see your first patient in somewhat uncomfortable clammy conditions. Each doctor had their preferred air-con setting. Whilst the New Zealand docs chose to have their rooms practically Arctic, those from Europe and Singapore liked things a little more temperate. We were answerable to a medical director, who was a virtual absentee, a practice manager, and an Australian owner who sold up half way through our time there, which resulted in a major negative knock-on effect.

There were normally three receptionists on duty at any one time, and plenty of nurses available for procedures. The nurses, and to some extent the doctors, were guided by our Senior Nurse Manager, who had worked with the company since the clinic first opened in 1999, and was the go-to member of staff for any questions we had.

Our clinic had staff from all over the world, but we never boasted about how inclusive we were. The diversity was so ever-present that it ceased to be an issue. Nobody thought about it or gave a toss. That, of course, is *real* diversity, as opposed to the politically correct, identity politics tripe that infects our public bodies *ad infinitum*. The NHS, by constantly fretting about diversity and inclusion, misses the point completely, which is to make sure you have enough staff to provide a decent service. The public's priorities are not the multicultural background of the staff that treat them, but the quality and speed with which they are treated.

The only unpleasant detail of my contract was the need to work Saturday mornings. I eventually negotiated this down to every other weekend, but scrapping Saturdays completely was out of the question. Saturday is a working day in Singapore, so much so that if a public holiday falls on a Saturday, you do not get a day off *in lieu*. Our clinic opened from nine till one on a Saturday, which does not sound like much, but the four hour clinics were normally rammed full of patients who were unable to get in during the week due to work commitments. This generated plenty of paperwork at the end of the clinic, meaning you rarely got home before three.

My Saturday mentality was never the best, especially with stroppy patients. I loathed buggering up my weekend and ended up resenting being at work in the first place, as if I was doing *them* a favour. Your Friday night was also downgraded from a relaxing, unwinding evening, into a normal work night. It was heartbreaking to walk home amongst the palm trees and expat pubs, seeing people kicking back, loosening their ties and downing their cold beers. You also found yourself too knackered to enjoy Saturday, drinking too much and wiping out Sunday with a hangover, before getting an early night and returning to the same sodding routine, week after week, month after month.

With the same weather almost every day, except for the couple of months of rainy season and the couple of weeks of haze in the summer, life can get somewhat monotonous in Singapore. The quality of life may be amazing, but the work-life balance is not.

By international standards, our fees were not high. A standard private appointment cost approximately forty UK pounds, based on the exchange rate at the time. Depending on the complexity or length of the appointment, the doctor could charge more. We also carried out some 'screening medicals', but there was rarely more than one of those per day. These medicals could be quite lucrative, although they did involve extra paperwork. There were other ways to earn extra money in the practice, through procedures, such as skin tag or mole removal, and cryotherapy, used to freeze off warts, and ingrowing toenail removals and the like. All this helped build up your practice income.

Medicals, or 'Wellness' screening, have become a huge growth industry. There are two groups of patients who attend medicals: there are the patients who are there under sufferance, due to an employment or insurance obligation, who are happy to get the whole thing out of the way as soon as possible, and those at the other end of the spectrum, who booked and paid for the medical themselves, and who are consequently eager for the examination to be very thorough. In Singapore, as well as in London, various types of medical were available to suit different patients. Older patients tended to opt for a longer medical with a more detailed report.

'Wellness' is not the same as 'Screening'. Screening should fulfil a set of strict criteria: the tests must be sensitive, specific, and useful in diagnosing a disease early, with a provable effect on outcomes. A standard set of blood tests may not fulfil the criteria for screening. Due to the cost, screening on a national level, such as breast or cervical cancer screening, must pass stringent tests to show real benefits[64]. Even these programs are not without controversy, with many doctors and epidemiologists pointing out they do more harm than good.

General blood tests are problematic, as overdiagnosis can cause unnecessary anxiety, resulting in further investigations that may themselves have unwelcome consequences. Even worse are 'false negatives', when a normal blood test may not rule out disease, leaving the patient falsely reassured. If you are at higher risk of developing certain conditions, a doctor should carry out targeted tests and examinations using patient concern and clinical acumen to reach, or exclude, a diagnosis, thus uncovering asymptomatic conditions with a real bearing on patient health. This may be termed 'preventative medicine', and is highly important, especially in cost sensitive systems like the NHS, as prevention is so much cheaper than cure.

In the clinic I worked at in Singapore, bespoke medical checks were often a pleasant way of getting to know the expatriate patients and their interesting life stories.

Travel medicine was another huge part of our workload. The expatriate clinic was first founded twenty years previously as a 'general practice and travel clinic'. Although travel medicine does not always involve treating ill people, it is a very useful area of preventative medicine. South East Asia, North Asia and the Indian subcontinent were the main holiday destinations for our clientele, although top end African Safaris also featured. Standard vaccinations were hepatitis A and B, typhoid, and tetanus, with malaria and rabies prevention also being important. Patients would present with their yellow travel booklets and it was up to us to determine exactly what vaccines were needed, depending on age, itinerary and vaccination history. This could be surprisingly stressful, as there were no prizes for getting all the vaccines right, only complaints if you got anything wrong.

Travel consultations also involved post-travel advice if something had gone wrong. One family attended for post-exposure rabies vaccines following a trip to Goa in Western India, during which they were confronted on the beach by a rabid donkey that went berserk, biting all the tourists. A diarrhoea outbreak in a Bali hotel also caused great unpleasantness, as did a hurricane in the Philippines that resulted in a tetanus outbreak.

Our clinic forged links with many specialists over the years, and we developed an approved list of consultants for referrals. As most of our clientele had decent private insurance, the referrals were straight forward and efficient, with patients often being seen on the same day. Our referrals were mostly directed to the two nearby private hospitals, the – both very British-sounding – Mount Elizabeth, and Gleneagles.

In the UK, certainly in the NHS, any freebies or perks of the job have long since gone. When I started working as a GP for the NHS, it was not uncommon for a weekly drug company to sponsor one of our practice meetings, carrying out a short presentation and giving us pens, post-it notes, calendars and other trinkets, as well as paying for our lunch. One of my colleagues in secondary care was even flown business class around Europe and the USA, to sponsored conferences.

All of this is now history in the UK. Along with the onward march of political correctness and the general 'public equals good, private equals bad' sensibility, a strange ethical puritanism has taken hold. When I returned to the UK in 2017, such drug sponsored practice meetings, let alone more lucrative freebies, had all but vanished.

The Singaporean specialists, who were not short of a bob or two, took us doctors out annually to some of Singapore's best restaurants, often attached to five-star hotels. Here we knocked back high-quality wine while eating an expensive meal for free. Rather than trying to curry favour or gain an unethical advantage on their competitors, this was instead a way of thanking us for all the referrals we had sent them over the previous year. If it wasn't for the specialists' generosity, I wouldn't have been able to afford to dine in those establishments. Ethical considerations seemed somewhat unimportant as you knocked back a glass of delicious claret, or munched on a juicy fillet mignon. Perhaps there should be *some* perks to being a doctor, and being treated to an occasional meal is hardly the ethical dilemma some make it out to be. I do not think it affected any of our referral rates or changed our practice in the slightest.

Christmas gifts were a different matter. Due to the 'high end' nature of our clinic, and the affluence of some of the specialists, we were deluged with luxurious gifts, expensive wines, hampers, chocolates, pâtés, and cheeses. Unfortunately, management took a dim view of all of this and the doctors were each given only a couple of gifts from the communal pile. Management's ethics, however, did not extend to themselves and the 'backroom staff' were only too happy to make off with the lion's share of the booty. This seriously annoyed some of my Singaporean colleagues, for whom some consideration, especially at seasonal times of the year, was part of the local culture.

While applying for my job in Singapore, I was pleased to discover that patients from the UK would be making up a large chunk of my workload. I assumed that I would be able to bond with them, find out where they were from, and banter about Premier League football or Six Nations rugby. At the same time, I would understand their levels of expectation, having previously been both a doctor and a patient in the NHS. We would be speaking the same language of healthcare, if you will. But whilst the first point ran true, and establishing a cultural connection was generally easy, I turned out, on the second expectation, to be well wide of the mark.

The way newly arrived expatriates from the UK reacted to a high-end general practice clinic was very intriguing. Most of the patients had never used private GP services before. Such patients had one of two reactions, each utterly different, to having a British GP in front of them. The first was to regard their GP with zero respect whatsoever, possibly because their experience of NHS general practice was a rushed ten-minute appointment after a three week wait. The other reaction was moralistic, as having to pay for healthcare up-front seemed to be part of an evil capitalist plot to deprive them of what they were entitled to anyway.

'So, I suppose I have to pay for *that* as well', they would huff and puff, regularly querying our prices, giving the receptionists put-upon looks as they dug into their wallets. Pretty hypocritical, as most of the patients were very wealthy, far wealthier than the doctors who were treating them. They were also working in one the most capitalist places on earth, often in investment banks, so any accusations of being money-driven or greedy were more than a touch hypocritical.

The mere concept of being in a private clinic sometimes went to their heads completely. I am sure that most of the UK patients were very nice people, but some of them, the moment they passed through our doors, lost all grip of reality, proceeding to act as though they were in a five-star hotel and we were their servants.

The American attitude to healthcare, meanwhile, could not have been more different from that of the British. Healthcare, especially amongst the affluent community we served, was a commodity to be purchased. Medicine in the US, rather like religion, has much more of a market feel, partly because of the way prescription medicines are so aggressively marketed. Watch commercials in the states, and you will see endless adverts for medications, followed by exhortations to 'ask your doctor about' said medicine, followed by a rapid list of side effects (this was summed up brilliantly in *The Simpsons*, when a hair restorer commercial came with the warning, 'may cause loss of scalp and penis').

Even for minor conditions such as coughs and colds, American patients would expect some medication on prescription, whereas your average European or Aussie patient would simply get this from the pharmacy. The American faith in doctors was palpable: the US appears to venerate and respect its physicians far more than the UK. On the negative side, huge faith was also placed in the medicines themselves. If a recommended cough medicine did not work, the patient would be back within forty-eight hours to request an alternative.

Cough medicines have a poor evidence base. The cough is part of the body's defence mechanism. It releases viral particles into the air and clears the airway. This means that suppressing a cough, especially in children, can be counterproductive, an explanation that was often met with blank stares by US patients who, after a couple of consultations for a 'cough', would lose interest and demand the antibiotic prescription they felt they needed from the start. I once had a ten-year-old American patient's mother scream at me, as we had been unable to 'cure' her daughter's four-day old cough. In the NHS, such nonsense can be brushed off, but in our red-carpet private clinic the punters had to be kept happy or management would get frightfully upset. After couple of months seeing North American patients, many with little more than simple coughs and colds, I realised I had to meet their expectations. 'It's only a cold, it will get better by itself', would not wash. A more precise diagnosis backed up with medication would always be required.

I have described my experiences in the Expatriate Medical Clinic, but this is not typical of healthcare in Singapore. I should therefore touch on Singapore's own healthcare system as used by the locals and citizens.

Singapore's healthcare sector produces excellent results by any international comparison and *stratospheric* results when compared to the surrounding countries. Healthcare is paid for from several different sources, including a universal healthcare system run by the Ministry of Health[65]. The reliance on public subsidies is far less than other first world countries, as compulsory savings, national healthcare insurance, and top-up private insurance are all added to the pot, and the private sector is far larger than it is in the UK.

Medisave is essentially a medical savings account, forming part of the CPF (central provident fund), and is used for other purposes, too, such as retirement and mortgage payments. It is a compulsory deduction from the wages of the individual, whose contribution of twenty percent is then added to by the employer, who contributes seventeen percent. Medisave costs can also be pooled amongst family members.

Medishield is a basic insurance scheme, more of a safety net, and premiums can be paid out of Medisave accounts. The government provides premium subsidies to lower income residents and the elderly. *Eldershield* is a severe disability insurance scheme, which insures against, among other things, the cost of elderly private nursing homes. This scheme is part managed by private insurers. You can also pay into Medshield life to protect against catastrophic illness.

There is also a safety net program through '*Medifund*', which covers the lowest class of hospital fees and services, and is only available to individuals who have depleted their other medical savings accounts. However, this cannot be shared between families, so it is possible for an individual to be exposed to catastrophic expenses. Direct subsidies are also available for those warded in public hospitals. These are assessed based on the type of ward, as well as the patient's level of income. Means testing is carried out, but this depends on the services being used. Patients with no income have their subsidy rate tagged to the value of their home.

Healthcare is of an exceptionally high standard. Singapore is probably one of the best countries in the world in which to fall ill. The facilities I observed in both private and public hospitals were excellent. This is also borne out by the statistics, which show one of the lowest infant mortality rates in the world, long life expectancy, and high levels of patient satisfaction[66].

Unlike the US system, which, as well as being extremely expensive, has myriad gaps to fall into, the Singaporean system has both better coverage and is better value for money. The UK is at the other end of the spectrum: it is extremely expensive, more so than Singapore, but tries desperately hard to convince the public that the service is 'free'. The costs are, of course, hidden within general taxation. This notionally 'free' aspect is used to demonise alternative types of provision, private and public, even when these can also be free at the point of delivery.

Singapore's achievement in creating excellent outcomes for less money is admirable; such is the success of the model that many other countries study and try to learn from it, especially first world countries with ageing populations.

As discussed previously, the area in which the Singaporean system differs most from that of the UK is the ability to opt for different 'classes' of ward, ranging from 'A', with a private room with your insurance paying, or 'B' an open ward with a shared toilet, which is funded by both insurance and the state, to class 'C' where the government pays the lion's share.

The health system in Singapore epitomises the country itself: a technocratic, highly efficient, small state in control of a private based system, but very much in the background. Compulsory private insurance, like motor insurance in the UK, cuts down on costs and gives consumers of healthcare a more direct relationship to the funding and utility of their medical needs. The individual is empowered with more personal responsibility, and the state can take a more long-term, proactive approach to healthcare. This contrasts with the profoundly reactive approach of the behind the curve, poorly planned, and hyper-politicised NHS.

Lee Kwan Yew was certainly unimpressed by the NHS. During a trip to London a decade before he died, he fell ill whilst in the UK, and was taken to the Royal London Hospital in Whitechapel. He took one look at the place, the dirty, dark corridors, the fag smokers with their drip stands loitering outside the door, and the overworked staff rushing about with their NHS name tags attached to blue ribbons, and told his security staff to get him the hell out. Within hours, he was back on a Singapore Airlines jet, happy to take the risk of a thirteen-hour flight.

The Singaporean system would not work well in the US due to its coercive aspect in taking funds directly from the consumer's income. This is the problem with the *Affordable Care Act*, also known as Obamacare: mandating people to purchase health insurance is unpopular in the land of the free. For not entirely unjustified reasons, Americans do not like to be *mandated* to do anything.

The system in Singapore is certainly not perfect. The obvious problem is the risk of exposure to catastrophic costs. Although it happens relatively rarely, as most people take out extra cover, this can still occasionally bankrupt an entire family.

Singapore's small size, and highly competent, technocratic government allows for close control of health provision and provides for any possible change of direction if needed. Trying to change course and develop a more sustainable model of healthcare in the US, on the other hand, would be akin to trying to herd cats. In the UK, meanwhile, the brick wall of political consensus would immediately be hit, as would a preference for putting off difficult political decisions.

One of the reasons Singapore and many other newly developed countries do not follow the NHS model is the visible near-collapse of state funded social security schemes in Western countries. These schemes were originally designed as safety nets, but have now become universal entitlements. It then becomes difficult for governments to scale these systems back without fatally undermining their popularity. This has led to the West living beyond its means, borrowing great sums to finance its welfare states[67]. The US healthcare public liability is greater than any other. Despite the strongly held belief in the UK that the US has system with little taxpayer input, American healthcare and social security entitlements may one day bankrupt the entire country, although nobody really wants to admit it.

Countries like Singapore, when they look at our social security and healthcare systems, see states that are trying to provide a level of security that is simply not attainable in a globalised workplace. They see welfare systems with the perverse by-product of a situation in which one can earn more from 'benefits' than from an after-tax working income.

Singapore certainly does not have this problem. After the London riots of 2011, one of the healthcare assistants at the expatriate clinic asked me if the rioters had jobs: were they not worried that they might be sacked as a result of their involvement? I then had to explain the benefits system to her, a painstaking process. She literally did not believe me.

'You mean they pay people *not* to work?' She said with incredulity. 'Then why does anyone bother?'

An oversimplification, of course, but you get her point. Singapore, a young country (in terms of its founding, rather than its demographic), still retains a highly developed work ethic based on the memory of only a generation or two before, when if you did not work, you did not eat. It may be worth pointing out this still holds true for most of the world's population. Western countries are the exception, not the rule. To live without work, assuming that you are able bodied, or to live off the hard work of others, is unthinkable, and would incur a degree of social stigma. Yet in the West, the social security gravy train left the station so long ago that we have forgotten what life was like without it.

Trying to provide a welfare safety net is the mark of a civilised society. Few would disagree with that, whatever your political stripe. But to go far beyond that basic provision in the name of an unachievable equality is counterproductive. With healthcare no longer being tethered to any form of personal responsibility, and the invisible (but very real) taxpayer picking up the tab, there is no incentive to keep ballooning costs down. The demographic timebomb hitting ageing Western Europe, with its empty maternity wards and closing schools, means taxpayers will be fewer and more sharply taxed than ever before. The welfare system will collapse under its own weight, unless the international money markets are happy to continue to finance huge government borrowing at low cost, thus dumping the burden onto future generations. Freedom will be squeezed in the name of equality.

I look back on my time in Singapore with great affection. If travel broadens the mind, my experience as an expat stretched it to its widest limit. I learned more about my own country, rediscovering a certain pride in our history. Britain once led the world in many areas, but has since been overtaken by some of its former colonial outposts, as well as the wider world in general. Singapore is a unique experiment, not just in healthcare but many other facets of life, and its huge success should repay close analysis.

The NHS needs urgent reform. This can only be achieved with an open mind. We must take an evidence-based approach to see what works best for staff and patients alike. This cannot be done with a rigid mindset. Singapore started its health system (and country) from ground zero. We may need to do the same. This is not, however, to advocate a system that involves up-front costs and anxiety for patients. We will still need some type of National Health Service, just not the national blind spot that is *the* National Health Service at present. It will not be an easy journey, but it will be worthwhile.

In the UK, we have the privilege of living in a desirable country, one that many people from far flung countries are desperate to get into. We should therefore ask ourselves why so many healthcare professionals are desperate to get out. To simply think that we can resolve this by tinkering with the current system, or by implementing only modest reforms, is a delusion.

9. AUSTRALIA
Splendid Isolation

In the Seventeenth and Eighteenth centuries Britain had a surfeit of population; nowhere better illustrated than in its teeming and overcrowded prisons; too many criminals and lots of ne'er do wells with nowhere to send them. The American Colonies across the Atlantic Ocean were a principal destination for many of those on the periphery of society, where criminals could be sold into indentured servitude and got rid of, along with those who travelled voluntarily to the New World.

Eventually this rebounded badly on the British. Large amounts of land and a more meritocratic society meant that by the 1770's the populations of the colonies were richer, freer, and more prosperous than the homeland (if you were white that is). The British fought off the French in North America with the help of the colonials and thus enjoyed hegemony over the whole of the Eastern Seaboard, from Florida to Canada. Not unreasonably the British sought to tax the colonials to help pay for the ruinous costs of this war. This is where the wheels came off. A surprisingly enlightened and learned group of men, later immortalized as the 'Founding Fathers' were able to seize upon the maxim 'no taxation without representation', which dates from 1765, and generate popular discontentment with the mother country, resulting in conflict, war, and secession. It was not easy but by 1781 the colonial forces managed to extract a sufficiently high price in blood and treasure from their erstwhile protectors to be left alone to independence. They created a federal entity which they named the *United States of America*, a country of which you may have heard.

This left the British with something of a quandary. All these convicts and nowhere to send them. Other parts of the Empire, such as Bengal or the Caribbean were problematic as they had their own pre-existing populations. What they needed was somewhere empty of civilization, if this meant painting a bit more of the world imperial pink, well that was no bad thing.

After the remarkable explorations of Captain James Cook of Middlesborough, a colony was founded at Botany Bay in 1788 and which he named 'New Wales', later amended to 'New South Wales'. Over the next century, multiple other colonies were founded on the 'Australian' continent. The white settlers encountered limited and sporadic resistance from the local Aboriginals tribes, who either retreated inland or co-existed with the settlers; demoralised, depressed, subjugated, and decimated by diseases against which they had no protection.

In 1901 the colonies federated together as a new country – the Commonwealth of Australia. Despite its unpromising origins, Australia has developed into a country of extraordinary affluence, with one of the highest standards of living in the world. Its sunshine and prosperity have attracted new waves of emigration, so that alongside the continual flow of British and Irish settlers, there came waves of other Europeans, followed by Chinese, Vietnamese, and Indians, all of whom helped to create a vibrant and successful country.

My family and I decided to move to Australia in 2018. It was initially an open-ended plan, but, after two and half years, the pandemic and its border controls forced us back to the UK, although we would have liked to stay longer.

British GPs are classed as IMGs (International Medical Graduates). This means that, when working abroad, they normally need to work in an 'area of need'. Working in a private practice in central Sydney or Melbourne would not, therefore, be possible. Tasmania or Western Australia, however, were options. After looking at all the possibilities, we decided to go for Perth, the capital of Western Australia.

The Australian healthcare system varies a great deal, not only from state to state, but also from region to region and town to town. The huge areas that lie outside Australia's state capital cities mean that rural medicine is very different from city medicine. A friend who worked in Queensland would be flown to towns five hundred miles away to run a clinic for the weekend. The duties of GPs practicing in the outback, especially in indigenous communities, can include delivering babies and cutting out appendices.

Western Australia is enormous, bigger than the whole of Western Europe. Apart from the coast, however, and the south western corner, it is virtually uninhabitable. Most of the state's population therefore live in Perth. A glance at a map will give an idea of just how far Perth is from anywhere else. It is the most isolated city in the world, not just from other countries, but within Australia itself. From a distance, the city appears to be a skyscraper metropolis, with an impressive skyline. When you get closer, however, the reality is that Perth is a big country town, feeling more like a collection of suburbs than an urban metropolitan area.

Perth and its surrounding cities and suburbs spread north to south along the coast, never venturing far inland. Some of the beaches are stunning and remarkably unspoiled. Given the westward coastline, one is also privileged to some of the most incredible sunsets in the world as the big yellow ball dips rapidly into the Indian Ocean. Great White Sharks cause the occasional scare and their proximity to the shore results in many injuries, although rarely fatalities. Before Western Australia existed, it was the 'Swan River Colony', and the river still forms the centrepiece of the Perth cityscape; its notable Black Swans being the emblem of the state and appearing on the State Flag.

The climate has more hours of sunshine that any other Australian Capital City, but frosts can occur in the middle of winter. The main weather hazard is excess heat. During our two summers, the mercury hit forty-three degrees. The wind can be a bit of a pain, the 'Fremantle Doctor' blowing in from the sea causing unsecured hats and sandwiches to end up tossed around on the sand.

My place of work was to the north of the city centre, in a new suburb known as Madeley. Here, the huge houses with pools that we had come to recognise as a feature of WA were intermixed with poorer accommodation, and some trailer parks. As mentioned above, this was an 'area of need', one in which IMGs could work easily.

The process of going to live and work in Australia, for doctors – and, I assume, for many other professionals – was time consuming and expensive. Nevertheless, after going through several months of this painstaking process, our visa came through.

When I arrived at my place of work, the first thing I noticed was that of the other eight GPs working in the clinic, only one was Australian. Of the rest, one was Irish, and six were British. This latter group, most of whom had made the move in the previous two years, all said they left because of disillusionment with the NHS, and had no intention of going back. This was a pattern amongst the British doctors I met on various training courses. How much it cost the British taxpayer to train us all, I dread to think. It was clear that a great number of doctors had been so overworked by the National Health Service that they had simply voted with their feet and buggered off. There were whole Medical Centres in WA run and staffed by Pommie doctors, prepared to travel over eight thousand miles for a better quality of life.

There was no delusion here, no slavish devotion to the founding principles of the NHS. Those who are prepared to take a risk and work internationally tend to be less insular than their counterparts back home, who continue to be fed a daily diet of NHS worship from the mainstream media.

These were all fantastic, hard-working doctors, with excellent clinical ability. They were amongst the best GPs I have ever worked with. For the UK, it is a great shame that some of its finest clinicians feel unable to continue in their home country. I thought of desperately understaffed primary care facilities in the UK who would greatly benefit from doctors like these. It is bad enough when your country doesn't train enough doctors and is forced to recruit from overseas, but it is unforgivable to compound your recruitment shortfall by letting your best doctors slip through your fingers. Surely this is a devastating indictment of how the NHS is run?

So how does the system in Australia work? Many people go private without any of the associated stigma we see in the UK. Private insurance is considered neither rarified, nor unaffordable, as it is in the UK. But the private side of things is not what we are examining.

Medicare is the government-provided health system. It is paid for by taxation, however, unlike in the UK, it is not paid for through general taxation. Instead, a separate surcharge appears on tax returns. If you have taken out private insurance, this reduces your Medicare surcharge, so you do not pay twice over. Something similar used to be the case in the UK, as private medical insurance was tax deductible. But this was done away with by the last Labour government in a fit of egalitarianism, thereby putting private healthcare out of reach for even more people, reducing choice, and forcing the public to use the NHS. As a GP, I was a self-employed contractor. In this case, that meant no holiday pay, no sick pay, and no protection. Unlike in Singapore, where I was an employee, there was no minimum pay per month. Every single bit of my income was derived from seeing patients. I received no money for carrying out diagnostic tests or prescribing medications, so there was little chance of abuse of the system.

The upside of being self-employed was that you could work as much or as little as you wanted. As a standard rule of thumb, a full-time doctor worked about forty hours a week. This worked out as roughly eight hours a day, spread over five days, or ten hours a day, spread over four days. You were expected to cover alternate weekends, which was a nuisance, though this normally entailed working on either Saturday or Sunday, rather than both.

The medical conditions and workload were broadly similar to the UK, although there was the occasional Aussie-specific injury, such as a red back spider bite, or a snake bite, which would result in a call to the venom hotline. Overall, the patients were younger and healthier than those in the UK. Though obesity and diabetes were less prevalent issues than they are in the UK, a looming obesity epidemic means that WA is probably not far behind. Alcohol abuse seemed to be more of an issue than it is back home, and mental health problems were just as prevalent. There were many British and South African patients, as well as a surprising number of Kiwis. We also had a sprinkling of Aboriginal patients, who had rather different healthcare needs to those of the general population. A few of the patients were miners who worked a long way away from Perth, the nature of their work giving rise to the acronym FIFO (fly in, fly out). Overall, we were welcomed, and there was not much of the abrasive anti-Pommie rudeness and sneering that I had previously encountered during a trip to Queensland.

As a new doctor, I was fully booked almost immediately. Standard appointments lasted fifteen minutes, so on an eight-hour day you would, in theory, have about thirty-two appointments. This was rarely the case, however, as patients would often book half hour appointments for mental health checks or 'care plans', and you would normally have two fifteen-minute-long coffee breaks, one in the morning and another in the afternoon. It could be a bit of a slog, but there was little admin, and the processing of patients was so efficient, that you would never leave late, unless there were exceptional circumstances, and you certainly never had to log on from home to work remotely. There were no home visits, as these were all done by a separate agency. Within your competence level, you could do as much minor surgery as you liked. We had two excellent practice nurses who were able to work independently. Our phlebotomist was on-site for bloods, and we had physiotherapists, chiropractors, counsellors, and even a large radiology unit next door, which was a separate business, offering walk-in services for X-rays, and MRI/CT and Ultrasound scans by appointment.

The job was very easy to get the hang of. The main area that an NHS émigré would need to get used to is billing. The other issue was one of accessibility, of which there was rather a surplus. As there were more GP appointments than there were patients, there was no barrier to making an appointment to see a doctor. In the NHS, there is a hassle factor regarding this, but in WA anyone could book for anything, which could result in having to see patients for very minor coughs and colds. A day filled with this sort of patient was both unfulfilling and poorly re-numerated, as basic consults such as these could be had for a minimal fee.

The patient experience was as different from the NHS as it is possible to be.

In WA, the local clinics were in direct competition for patients, rather than the other away round. Patients could usually see a doctor of their choice on the day they booked, and even if we were full, they had the option of seeing a doctor in a nearby practice if needed. Unlike the NHS, patients in Australia can be registered at several different practices. Walk-in patients were almost all seen straight away, especially if they were children. If a Medicare bulk-billing practice (where all or most of the patient fees are billed in bulk to Medicare, so the service is mostly free at the point of delivery) was unavailable, there were also plenty of private GPs around who were able to see patients for a reasonable price, even at weekends.

Witness the complete reverse in mentality: unlike an NHS surgery, where being overwhelmed is a disaster for patients and a source of hand-wringing for under-resourced practices, in an Australian practice you end up bemoaning having to turn people away. This is not because they add to your workload, but because you lose income. The GP practices are hungry for patients. If their existing doctors are fully booked, they simply recruit more, who rapidly pay for themselves by being able to see, and charge for, the surplus patients. This phenomenon is called supply and demand.

Australians are also far more likely to have private medical insurance than their counterparts on the UK. Roughly half the population has private medical insurance in some form or another, and this rises to seventy percent in Western Australia[68]. This means that if a local good quality bulk billing Medicare GP is available nearby, patients will use that service, while using their private cover for hospital treatment, mainly to ensure a shorter waiting time for outpatient or inpatient consultant led care. From a primary care point of view, it did not make a huge difference to us whether people were privately covered or not, as we were billing 'Medicare'.

One huge advantage of the Australian system is the speed of diagnostics. Our blood tests were processed rapidly. We were also able to refer patients for imaging very quickly. If a patient needed, for example, an MRI on a possible anterior cruciate injury to the knee, I was able to pick up the phone and book the scan myself. If the radiology practice next door was completely overrun with patients, which rarely happened, the patient may have had to wait a day or two, at most. By comparison, I was working in an NHS practice recently when one of the GPs said how impressed he was that a patient he referred for an MRI had been given an appointment within three weeks. And his surprise was completely well founded. Three weeks in the NHS is very good. But God, we have set the bar low!

The Australian system is not perfect, however. Medicare does let some patients down, such as those without private insurance, who must wait a long time for ENT appointments, and a few who are on long waiting lists for surgery.

'Aha!' you might say, 'so there *are* problems with the system, maybe the NHS is not so bad after all'. But wait, I said *some* patients: yes, a small minority can end up with long waits for treatment, but in terms of both numbers and waiting times the NHS is vastly worse.

Although Medicare is similar to the NHS in terms of its cover, it is not *directly* funded by government. All primary care facilities are, therefore, essentially privately run businesses. They are sometime owned by doctors, although they can be owned by pharmacists, non-clinicians, or large corporations. Unlike a standard UK partnership arrangement, in which the practice is funded by a lump sum from the government, known as the global sum, and can make up to ten percent of its income from private sources, in Australia the practice will claim a fee from Medicare for any patient it sees. All patients must therefore have a Medicare number in order to be properly billed. Doctors must likewise have a Provider number.

All services can be billed together, starting at a level 'A' consultation, which is about thirty-seven dollars (roughly twenty GB pounds), up to a much lengthier consultation, which would incur a greater fee. Care plans and more detailed arrangements involving other services, such as physiotherapy or podiatry, will incur much higher fees. This does encourage GPs to be more creative and channels incentives towards those who need it most. Seeing patients with chronic conditions, for example, pays far better than seeing ones with simple coughs and colds. Billing incentives are also available for out of hours services and for treating indigenous Australians.

It is likely that in somewhat poorer areas, there will be more bulk-billing practices as patients are less likely to rely on their private insurance, whereas in richer areas where patients have more coverage, you might expect more mixed-billing practices (where the practice has both Medicare and private patients) or solely private practices.

This leads to a huge amount of choice for patients, but also for doctors, who, provided they are Australian, can work anywhere in the country they wish.

The billing status of the practice did not, in my experience, make an obvious difference to the state of the practice itself. It was not as if there were swanky premises for the private docs and lousy ones for the Medicare ones. They were indistinguishable. And the free market ensured that costs were kept down. My wife, who did not qualify for Medicare as her home country did not have a reciprocal agreement with Australia, needed to see a GP a couple of times during our stay. The cost was sixty to ninety dollars for a standard appointment (about thirty-five to fifty pounds). This is far cheaper than the going rate to see a private doctor in the UK.

As for the NHS, the 'envy of the world', nobody mentioned it, and on the rare occasions they did, it was along the lines of 'at least we don't have your system'.

Most of this chapter is directly related to my personal experience in primary care, but we did have one experience of hospital care. My wife, who was somewhat accident prone at the time, managed to break her ankle on one of the strange sloping kerbs that line the pavements in WA. This caused a minor break. We had to go to the nearest A&E, which was located in the northern suburb of Joondalup. As this happened at the beginning of our stay, we were nervous: we had not yet managed to get her health insurance sorted out.

On arrival in A&E, I had, rather awkwardly, to sign a waiver stating that I agreed to pay, whatever the fee was. Our experience, it must be said, was akin to an A&E visit in the UK. It was a Saturday night, and we had to wait a long time amongst the usual assortment of drunks and idiots. My wife was called through for an initial assessment by a nurse, then had another wait to see a doctor, before finally undergoing an X-ray. There were all the familiar hallmarks of an A&E in the NHS: strip lights, vending machines, and dodgy toilets. In all, we were there for about six hours. Throughout, I nursed an unholy dread of my wife needing surgery, which, given that we were uninsured, would have cost thousands of dollars. In this sense, I have sympathy for all those who are uninsured and unable to access health care free at the point of delivery.

You may be tempted to conclude that this dread of paying means that the NHS is automatically the better system.

But that would be misguided. My wife, being from neither Australia or the UK, was in a very unusual situation. (My two children and I were all UK citizens, meaning that we qualified for Medicare and would have had all emergency costs covered.)

It may not be always be apparent, or indeed be enforced, but the same situation that affected by wife also applies in the UK. If you are not expecting to be resident in the UK for six months or more, then you should be presented with a bill at the end of your treatment, whether you have been to an A&E department or a local GP surgery. This is a matter of fact, not opinion.

The difference with the Australian system is that they enforce this rule, whereas we do not, which leads to hundreds of millions of pounds of extra cost every year. UK taxpayers, therefore, end up paying for the medical care of those who arrive on our shores temporarily, and then either cannot or will not pay.

Partly for principled libertarian reasons, previous attempts to introduce ID cards in the UK have failed. But some sort of NHS card would, surely, be reasonable. After all, everyone who is entitled to NHS care has a unique NHS number. If we all had some form of 'NHS ID card', it could be produced on demand.

If the patient is not entitled to free NHS care, then they should pay. It is not obvious why this is so controversial, especially as it preserves at least *some* link between the taxpayer who pays for the service and those who are entitled to use it.

My wife's experience typifies that awful moment, one many tourists will recognise, when a health problem arises and your immediate thought is how you are going to pay for it.

The scale of Australia, which is also a continent, is difficult to process. In Western Australia in particular, rural communities exist huge distances from each other. To be a doctor providing care to a rural or disadvantaged indigenous population is not a popular vocational choice. This is why the salaries for doing so are very high, an example of supply and demand that has disappeared as a recruitment concept in the NHS, much to its detriment. GPs in the UK are often be paid the same, or even less, for working in a deprived area, which is quite extraordinary for a healthcare system that prides itself on universal care and equality.

The same also applies to nurses and other allied professionals. They will go where the work is, as you would expect if you were paid by how much work you did, or by the number of patients you saw, rather than at a flat rate.

Recently, I have noted many articles in newspapers complaining that Australia deliberately targets UK trained doctors by offering larger salaries and advertising the better weather and lifestyle. Annoyance is directed both at the recruiters themselves, and at doctors who take the bait. The line is clearly that, seeing as doctors and nurses have had their training on the NHS, it is ungrateful of them to then head abroad in search of more money or a better lifestyle.

This is palpable nonsense. It is up the NHS to become more attractive and raise its game, rather than expecting other countries to modulate their 'pull factors'. It is also grossly hypocritical of the UK to moan about this, given that the country is more than happy to poach third world doctors who were not only trained abroad, but whose skills are also desperately needed at home.

It is true that the UK can (just about) cope with its own doctors leaving by recruiting further down the food chain, but this luxury is not open to Sub-Saharan Africa or poorer parts of the Indian subcontinent, where the loss of domestically trained doctors can literally be a matter of life and death.

There is no point blaming doctors for this, either, who are highly qualified and intelligent, and have every right to put their skills forward in a globalised world. Doctors cannot be blamed for gravitating towards countries where they feel more valued on a performance level, and are better paid.

GP earnings in Australia were roughly comparable to those in the UK, at least for NHS partners, although in the former country GPs can, with a bit of elbow grease, vastly increase their incomes. Pensions in Australia, though, are less generous, and tax is roughly the same (i.e. high).

Australia is an expensive place to live. The UK doctors manning the GP surgeries I worked at had *not* travelled thousands of miles from home solely for financial reasons, which should tell you something. If we move to a system in which we train more of our own doctors, and are able to link pay closer to performance, the situation may well improve drastically. Most doctors who eventually choose to move abroad do not begin their careers with the expectation that they will relocate. But once they have been ground down by the NHS treadmill, who can blame them?

Whatever its issues, Australia does *not* have a health system in crisis. There are, of course, political differences between the major parties regarding Medicare payments and so on, but the Australian health care system is never, unlike the NHS, considered a national treasure, or used as an ideological football. Healthcare in Australia is not based on ideology but on a decision to prioritise good results. There is little clamour to reform the system, as is often the case in the US, or to protect it any form of free-market choice and competition, as there is in the UK.

The Aussies have built their healthcare system partly with British doctors. Over fifty percent of GPs working in Australia qualified in a different country, and many of these are from the UK[69]. There will always be a few doctors who are attracted to Australia's lifestyle and weather, but if the shocking level of staff turnover and mass emigration does not dispel the NHS delusion for you, I do not know what will.

10. ACROSS THE CHANNEL
The Champions' League

After the Second World War the countries of Europe were bankrupt and faced years of decline. They would no longer be the focus of world events in their own right, or exercise control over large global empires, but instead become proxies for the ideological Cold War between the United States and the Soviet Union.

As much of the pre-war economy and administration had been swept away, here was the perfect chance to start things from scratch. In healthcare, as we have discussed, the United Kingdom took a blueprint for an expanded welfare state, including contributory healthcare provisions (Beveridge) and effectively nationalised healthcare along socialist principles (Bevan). The Labour landslide of 1945 was primarily driven by the recognition the world had changed and the desire to try something new (as well as by troops who thought they would be demobilised more quickly) but there is little evidence that this represented a mass conversion to socialism amongst the population. It is interesting that of all the countries of Western Europe, the UK become the largest subscriber to a universal healthcare system provided for by general taxation. Perhaps because we had not been bombed back to the Stone Age, we thought we could afford it.

Other countries of comparable size did not follow our lead. Germany, which still refers to 1945 as year zero, had a completely blank canvas on which to paint. Nevertheless, it opted to retain the Bismarck-inspired system that had prevailed in the country since the 1880s, and has now evolved into one of the best healthcare systems in Europe. In Germany, public health insurance is mandatory; it is contributed to by both people and their employers[70]. This situation may be understood as similar to the one regarding motor insurance in the UK. Under the German system, everyone gets equal treatment; people can also put their children, and any other dependents, on their insurance.

Higher earners do not get better treatment, and insurance costs do not increase with age. The German system also has a parallel private insurance sector: if you earn above a certain amount, approximately fifty thousand pounds per year, you can opt out of the public system and get private insurance instead. This can be speedier, but does carry with it the usual snags of purely private insurance, such as not being covered for pre-existing conditions, and premiums getting higher with age. Approximately half the hospital beds in Germany are in public hospitals, about a third are not-for-profit, private beds, and a sixth are provided by for-profit private providers[71].

German public health insurance is recognised across the EU as being a more comprehensive system than most. Given the country's ageing population, costs are increasing, but they remain lower than those of other countries. Citizens can also have a combination of both public and private insurance, which can be tailored to their financial situation and medical needs. And yes, medical care is available equally to everyone, free at the point of need. Most Germans are very happy with their healthcare, with satisfaction scores being well over the OECD average[72]. Germany's healthcare system is also far better staffed than the NHS, with more doctors per head of population[73].

The system is not perfect, but because the attitude is different, and the Government is not expected to 'do things' or take sole responsibility, the system is far less politicised than the NHS. If something went wrong, you may direct your ire towards the hospital in which you were treated, or at your insurance company, rather than the government, or (yawn) the Tories. Germany has a mature, intelligent mixed system. Change could always take place, if needed, be it locally, at the state level, via the federal government in Berlin, or by the hospitals or providers themselves. Flexibility is in-built, and the system makes sure nobody goes without. This type of non-ideological solidarity is surely something we can learn a little from.

Let us now look at the French healthcare system, which is often rated the best in the world[74]. Can any ideas can be pinched from a country that begins just twenty-one miles off the coast of Dover?

France was, initially, somewhat off the mark with its healthcare provision, partly due to doctors jealously guarding their private practices. Only after Germany's healthcare reforms of the late 1880's had been shown to promote better survival against deadly infections, especially tuberculosis, did France begin to move towards universal healthcare. Indeed, is has been suggested that France's population growth, which has been slower than that of Germany, may be a direct result of poor healthcare provision. The poor quality of the health of military recruits acted as a major spur to change, in the same way it did in Britain. That, and all the existential issues that arose from it in an era of mass armies and the ever-shifting European balance of power.

In France today, as with many countries in Europe, the entire population must pay for compulsory health insurance[75]. These funds are then available to cover most healthcare needs. The system was partly inspired by the Beveridge Report, but the contributory principle was retained, unlike in Britain.

How interesting that France, a country with generally higher levels of state spending and a more Social Democratic economic model than the UK, has been completely outflanked on the left by the UK in this regard, both in a practical and ideological sense.

When seeking a doctor in France, there may be an upfront fee, but between seventy and one hundred percent of this fee is then reimbursed to the patient. The amount reimbursed is higher when costs are greater, for example for the treatment of more chronic medical conditions. The situation in France is similar to that of Germany: roughly three fifths of hospital beds are public, one fifth is provided by not-for-profit private companies, and another fifth by private for-profit companies[76]. Some moderate waits to see specialists do exist, but again the figures pale into insignificance compared to those in the UK. NHS style waiting lists would simply not be tolerated on a large scale in France.

The French government does have a role in overseeing health insurance funds and public hospitals, and in fixing the rates of medical expense. Nevertheless, healthcare in France is less centrally run and is far more flexible than it is in the UK.

Again 'solidarity' comes up. The more ill you are, the less you pay: a serious health condition and increased dependence will lead to full re-imbursement. It should also be pointed out that any fees not covered by mandatory insurance can be covered by a wide range of private complementary insurance plans. There is a very competitive market for these private plans, and market forces help keep the costs down. These plans are also often subsided by employers, so premiums are modest. This means that the majority of French people benefit from complimentary health insurance[77]. Patients on a low income are also covered by a solidarity top-up insurance.

The principle of compulsory insurance is at the heart of the system, but unlike in the US, this is normally state rather than private insurance. To be sure, there are inefficiencies, and there is some over-regulation due to bureaucracy, but this is nothing compared to the weak planning and performance of the NHS in the UK.

The Netherlands is another country with excellent healthcare outcomes, and it achieves them despite spending less on healthcare than either France or Germany. Dutch healthcare is ranked very highly among developed countries, always reaching the top three, and frequently being put in the number one spot[78].

Healthcare insurance in Holland is mandatory, and is funded through two different insurance schemes, one for long term illness, and another for day-to-day care. Affordability is guaranteed through income allowances, and risk is pooled, so having more illnesses does not lead to a higher premium. Unlike in many other healthcare systems in Europe, the Dutch

Government is responsible for access and quality, but *not* for the management of the healthcare sector.

In Spain, healthcare is less centralised than it is in the UK, and there is a large private sector, one which comprises almost thirty percent of health spending[79]. Parts of Spain have very impressive numbers of medical staff, some of the highest in the EU[80]. Healthcare in Spain, by the standards of most comparable countries, is regarded as extremely efficient .

In 1978, the Italian government established the SSN (*Servizio Sanitario Nazionale,* or National Health Service). The system is not quite the same as that of the UK, however, as healthcare is provided by a mixed public-private system, one that is administered on a regional basis. Italy's healthcare system is frequently ranked almost the best in the world, and the country has excellent life expectancy[81]. Italy's spending on healthcare as a percentage of GDP is also significantly less than that of Germany and France.

Every health system has its flaws, some being more obvious than others. We do not have time, however, for a detailed analysis of every healthcare system in the world, and such an analysis would make for a very dry book. Nonetheless, it is telling that while elements of the NHS have found their way into other healthcare systems in Europe, it has not been imitated on a large scale.

As chapter twelve will show, if you are preprepared to open your mind to consider empirical evidence of healthcare outcomes, then any further contention that the NHS is the 'best' system means you may be guilty of wishful thinking.

11. ALL AROUND THE WORLD
Different strokes for different folks

Let us consider a few different healthcare models, starting with the most statist, and then progressing to those with no state input whatsoever. (Let me add that this is not an exhaustive list by any means: many healthcare systems would fall between two options).

1. Complete state control of all healthcare, both supply and demand. No individual choice, with private healthcare either illegal or non-existent.
2. State control of healthcare, both the funding of it (via taxation), and the running of it. Private healthcare is rarified, and not accessible to the vast majority of the population, due to high costs, or it being non-existent, especially in poorer areas.
3. Universal healthcare funded by the state but run independently of it, and largely free from day-to-day political control. Access to private healthcare also available to a degree.
4. Universal healthcare generally underwritten by the state, but with a large minority of the population having some form of private healthcare.

5. A mixed-payer system, with both a state and private sector of roughly the same size, existing in parallel.
6. Healthcare is provided by compulsory private insurance, though it is underwritten by the state in certain circumstances, and through certain schemes.
7. Healthcare is guaranteed and funded by the state, but only in certain circumstances, and it only covers certain portions of the population.
8. The state provides a safety net of healthcare for emergency medicine. Most of the population are forced to rely on private means for anything beyond this, such as ongoing out-patient care.
9. Basic facilities only for the general population. Any healthcare, including calling an ambulance, draws a private fee, and is therefore only an option for a small number of the population
10. The state provides almost no medical care. Completely private self-payer system. Only elites can afford healthcare and facilities of any note are based in the capital city.
11. No healthcare safety-net, either state or private, of any kind, apart from international charities and aid organizations. Persons of wealth seek medical care outside the country.

Healthcare systems such as those described from nine to eleven are generally only seen in developing countries. Most developed countries provide a safety net for the health of their population; indeed, this often cited a yardstick for a civilised country, no matter what its internal history or culture. In theory, however, very rich countries could also have minimal cover, with a free market for healthcare that pushes prices down.

Where would certain countries around the world fit on this list? Number one is tricky to evaluate, as is covers mega rich countries, such as Brunei, but also somewhat historically poorer states, such as former Eastern Bloc countries and the Soviet Union. It does not automatically follow that such care is bad, as outcomes are often opaque. Indeed, in parts of the Soviet Union's history large leaps forward were achieved in healthcare. Other modern examples of number one include Cuba, and North Korea (where, theoretically, everyone has access to healthcare, but the quality is poor).

The UK's NHS would come out as number two on this list, and is therefore something of an outlier in Western Europe. Whilst the Netherlands may be best represented by number three, Most Western European systems are number four or five. Australia is best described by number five. Number seven on the list would probably account for the US system, although 'Obamacare' may, in theory, also nudge the US into number six, a category that would also include Singapore. Many African or war-torn Middle-Eastern countries would fall under numbers ten or eleven.

This illustrates the fact that the UK system does not represent a moderate compromise, existing in the centre of the political and ideological healthcare spectrum. In reality, in a global context, at least, it sits somewhere towards the extreme.

The US system sits far more in the middle than you might assume, given the vitriol that is poured onto American healthcare by the left.

The weirdest claim is that, without the NHS, people would be 'thrown out onto the streets, like in America', whatever that means. There is, in fact, a US federal law mandating emergency treatment free at the point of delivery for those who need it, called the Emergency Medical Treatment and Active Labour Act, EMTALA[82].

The US system is both utterly different and yet surprisingly similar to our own. It is similar in the sense that healthcare delivery is also highly politicised and heavily state funded (the federally mandated programmes *Medicare* and *Medicaid* were set up in the sixties, during the expansion era of Lyndon B. Johnson's 'great society' and 'war on poverty'). And yet the US system is different in its huge variety of healthcare delivery, as you would expect from a more market-based, individualist country that is comprised of states with very different laws, taxes, and public services.

The main cost difference is 'pricing'. Doctors earn significantly more money in the US compared to other countries, and there is a much greater cost of administration, especially relating to insurance. The *per capita* spend on pharmaceuticals is also much higher than it is elsewhere, and the cost of individual tests and services are also higher. A CT or MRI scan, for example, costs far more in the US than in most other developed nations.

There are upsides. Pharmaceuticals are more expensive due to higher investments and more innovation: in 2016, the US accounted for over half the global production of new chemical entities. Long waiting times are much less of a problem in the US than comparable countries, and the US has among the best record of any country when it comes to treating heart attacks and strokes.

It is also likely that big salaries boost performance and increase morale and staff retention. And, seeing as there is no universally acknowledged amount that doctors and nurses should be paid, who is to say that the US pays them too much, whilst we in the UK pay them far too little?

Cost has its problems, especially regarding accessibility. Some people miss an appointment because they cannot afford it, and around ten percent of Americans have no health insurance at all. There are holes in the US healthcare system, or systems. It is far from perfect, just as our NHS is far from perfect, but again, can we learn something from it, or is our system *so* perfect that with a bit more money everything would be fine? Rather than simply spending more and more on the same system, perhaps we should look at how the US and other countries manage their health care, copy the good ideas and reform the NHS, but there is no political will to do this.

People think they own the NHS, 'our NHS', as politicians universally rabbit on about at election time. Well, you do not own the NHS. The state does. The NHS is centrally owned, planned, and funded. If there was a big difference between political parties' policies for the NHS then you could exercise some degree of control via the ballot box, but they all say the same thing, so you cannot.

The Government does not act according to *your* needs, but the needs of the population. This is why, when you get your NHS hospital appointment through the post, or to your phone if you are lucky, it is at a time of the *hospital's* convenience, not yours. The government, if it is even vaguely fiscally competent, has an incentive to keep costs down due to the other budgetary demands placed upon it. State planning necessitates a reduction of choice, as the NHS is intended to be sole provider. When your competition is free, most private providers cannot not compete, so they are forced to charge far more, and private medicine becomes a small, elite endeavour.

When looking at healthcare models all over the world, from fully private to mixed systems, we are on the extreme, whether you like it or not. This is not to say anyone who supports the NHS is an extremist, but the UK health system does represent an ideologically extreme form of state control over health. This is not a party-political point. In the UK *all* major political parties support the NHS in its current form, and even favour doubling down on it; increasing spending and postponing difficult decisions.

At the centre of the NHS inability to innovate and modernise is a failure of forward-thinking about future demands on the service, and how needs can be met in a sustainable way based on resources available. To return to the far-sighted way Singapore runs its health service compared to the UK, it is a useful analogy to compares their respective national airports.

Heathrow Airport used to be the busiest international airport in the world. No longer. For the last few years Heathrow has been superseded by the monster that is Dubai International. In a few years Heathrow will drop out of the list of the world's top ten busiest international airports. One of the airports overtaking it will be Singapore's Changi. For the last couple of decades Heathrow has been effectively full, at over ninety-eight percent capacity (remind you of anything?).

As many passengers who use the airport regularly will know, with a capacity that high it only takes something small to go wrong; a failure of a check in service, bad weather or a baggage handlers' strike and the whole operation grinds to a halt, much to the frustration and misery of the public and the bewilderment of unimpressed foreigners.

This could have been avoided. Any study of patterns of aviation, especially the growth of no-frills fares or budget airlines, would easily have foreseen a huge increase in required capacity. But no, Heathrow was allowed to get more and more full. It is a tribute to the professionalism of air traffic control that tightly packed aircraft movements pass year on year with no serious accidents.

Changi Airport is owned by the Singapore state and this technocratic government has planned for the future. The current capacity will be doubled in just over a decade. The planning is proactive; the airport was never allowed to become full to bursting. This is reflected in the quality of the experience for customers, who vote Changi the world's best airport year after year[83].

This is not necessarily an argument for more runways or a bigger Heathrow; the much mocked 'Boris Island' idea for a new airport in the Thames estuary had the potential to be a spanking new, highly impressive facility to welcome the world to the UK, but a combination of environmental activism and national pessimism caused the prospect to be sneered at and discarded. Therefore, nothing gets done. Ever.

This is also not a 'free-market-is-best' argument as Singapore's airport is nationalised, while Heathrow airport is privately owned (by a Spanish company as it happens). One airport proactively plans for the future and never rests on its laurels. The other airport is profoundly reactive, constantly bursting at the seams, is easily thrown into disarray, and constantly playing catch up. As soon as a new terminal is built, capacity has already been reached and a new terminal is needed. The new facilities are obsolete from day one.

The same can be said of potholes in the road. How many times in the UK do you drive down a road littered with potholes? When the potholes are filled, they are repaired one at a time, a quick fix leaving an ugly (and bumpy) patchwork of different shades of grey cement. Any rush job will do, it seems, even when the more radical step of resurfacing the road will prove cheaper in the long run. In six and a half years I do not recall seeing a single pothole in Singapore.

Even if one accepts the case that more government spending is always desirable (an erroneous assumption, as Singapore's outcomes are much better than England's with less money spent per head as a proportion of GDP, while the USA and Scotland have worse outcomes with more money), you are still left with the problems of NHS planning and competence.

This is not a matter of ideology. *Some* degree of planning is essential and it must be done with competence and compassion. It is for those who resist any changes to the NHS model to come up with evidence of either in the current system. It is not enough to say that the government is uniquely qualified to provide the National Health Service if alternative models in other countries work better.

In the UK there is also huge variance *within* the NHS, often referred to as a 'postcode' lottery, with great services in some parts of the country and far worse provision elsewhere. It would be easy to judge the NHS only by the best results, as its advocates often do; yet these are the same people who insist on the standardisation and monolithic structure of the service, so we should really judge it as one institution.

Singapore's healthcare system is widely admired, but countries with existing high levels of welfare infrastructure will find it difficult to copy. This does not mean we cannot learn from it. Some flaws are self-evident; nobody should be exposed to catastrophic healthcare costs in a civilised society and although this happens rarely, this a loophole that needs to be closed.

The British love for their NHS, whether fed by politicians to the public or the other way round, is rooted in a sense of fairness and equity. High quality care for all, free at the point of need and not based on ability to pay. Nothing wrong with that. The error come from thinking *only* government systems can provide this. Insurance based systems, both state run, and private, exist in almost every other Western country, including throughout the EU. None of these have a hyper-politicised service, literally 'weaponised' in the words of the Labour Party leader during the 2015 election campaign.

There is also a weird aversion to the private sector in the UK, despite it being vanishingly small compared to other first world countries. This attitude does not seem to extend to seeing an optician, an osteopath, or a dentist, for some reason. It may be a fear of the profit motive, but some of the best healthcare in the world is both private and not for profit, for example the world's largest medical facility, the huge Texas Medical Centre in Houston, is owned by a not-for-profit corporation[84].

Rather than a love for the NHS, what people seem to prefer

is the *idea* of the NHS. It sounds so noble and wonderful; the state takes care of all your medical needs. It becomes less cosy when your elderly relative spends eight hours dehydrating on a hospital trolley, or your son's child psychology appointment is set for eighteen months' time.

Even if a health service is funded primarily from general taxation, there are other ways to organise and deliver care within that system. It is delusional to suppose that *a* National Health Service must be *the* National Health Service.

12. LIES, DAMN LIES AND...
Statistics

In 2017, the Commonwealth Fund published a study of the healthcare systems of eleven developed countries, ranking the NHS at the top. The NHS was especially congratulated for care process and equity. This outcome was as headline grabbing as it was surprising to all concerned. The report was trumpeted by the NHS itself[85], and has subsequently been used by those on the left as proof of the good of the NHS as a healthcare system[86]. The Fund looked at health care systems again in 2021, and the NHS, that time around, did rather poorly. Unsurprisingly, this did not make the same headlines.

So how good is the NHS when looked at in an international context? Is it brilliant, crap, or somewhere in between? The answer is that it sometimes falls at either of those extremes, but, amongst developed countries, is more often somewhere in the middle.

For most of this book, we have tried to explore perceptions of the NHS, asking in particular why people have such a strange, and, at times, irrational view of it. At some point, however, we must bring up facts and figures, rather than assertions. Again, mercifully for you (and for me to be honest), there is no capacity in this book for an avalanche of statistics to prove, or disprove, the poor performance of the NHS. Given the space available, statistics would need to be cherry-picked and selective, which would rightly lead to accusations of bias.

However, some comparison based on hard evidence is needed. An argument cannot only rely on ideology and anecdote.

All healthcare systems are unique and all have their own limitations and problems. Cultures are different, as are rates of smoking, obesity, and different types of cancer, so exact comparisons are difficult. Likewise, league tables are best avoided, so these are only referenced when necessary to provide context. For example, international league tables often feature many tiny but affluent countries (especially around Europe) that skew the results. A large country that is a high performer on cancer survival, such as Germany, may only come tenth in a table of European countries for outcomes. But when that top ten includes Luxembourg, Lichtenstein, San Marino, Andorra, Monaco, Iceland and so on, we do not get the true picture.

I have tried, therefore, to compare the UK to the nearest equivalent countries: Germany, France, the USA and, given my own experiences, Singapore and Australia. We will look at a few major areas of healthcare, going from cradle to grave to see how the NHS bears up internationally, while, of course, using sources that are as trustworthy as possible.

Let us first look at child infant mortality. This is a sad but necessary measure to evaluate healthcare systems, as it illustrates caring for human beings at their most vulnerable. Any civilised society should put care of the vulnerable at the centre of healthcare. Fortunately, most developed countries *do* act this way: as would be expected, the big difference in the figures is seen in the comparison between developed and developing countries, rather than between first world healthcare systems (which make it no less sad, of course).

Using 'World Population Review', the results are not pretty reading for the UK. We come a rotten thirty-fifth, with a rate of 3.62, just above Poland[87]. The US would appear to have a remarkably high rate, although the source material does point out that the US uses very different criteria when classifying infant mortality, extending the time period to the first birthday.

Outside Europe, Australia is eight places ahead of the UK, while Singapore is *twenty-eight* places ahead of the UK, with a rate of 1.85. Although the differences in absolute numbers may appear small, the figures show that newborns in the UK are twice as likely to die as Singaporean newborns.

Moving onto childhood, another intervention we can measure is the rate of infant vaccination. Countries in the developed world give slightly different combinations of vaccines to infants, and often give them at slightly different ages. For example, the UK gives a Meningitis B shot, whereas Australia does not. Singapore gives the Chickenpox vaccine, whereas the UK does not. Exact comparisons are therefore difficult, but the best standard is probably that of the MMR vaccine. The main first world outlier is probably Japan, which gives the MMR vaccine as three different shots for each condition, possibly due to discredited claims about the vaccine causing autism.

We will use the World Atlas to measure vaccination rates for measles, which normally amounts to the same thing as MMR. Ninety-nine percent coverage is achieved by a veritable pick and mix of countries, including several wealthy states in the Middle East, as well as China, Cuba and, remarkably, Eritrea. Singapore comes in the seventies by world rank, with ninety-five percent coverage, the same as Australia. The UK is in ninety-sixth place, with ninety-two percent coverage[88]. This may seem high, but bear in mind that there are only one hundred and ninety-two countries listed, meaning that we are exactly halfway. At bottom of the list is Equatorial Guinea, on a depressing thirty percent.

Polio eradication is pretty much *de rigeur* in most of the world these days, meaning that the scourge of this horrible virus has almost been eradicated, save for a few pockets in countries with a religious fundamentalist disincentive to vaccinate, such as Nigeria, Afghanistan, and parts of Pakistan. Thankfully, the UK is free of polio, although at ninety-three percent coverage we are still behind France, Australia, and Singapore, countries that all have ninety-six percent coverage[89].

Let us move beyond childhood into the world of diagnostics. MRI (Magnetic Resonance Imaging) scanners are hugely useful tools. They can provide a host of diagnostic information without the associated exposure to radiation of a CT scan, or of multiple X-rays.

In the UK, one of the frustrations of primary care is that, apart from some unusual exceptions, GPs are not allowed to order these diagnostics tests. Contrastingly, GPs in Singapore and Australia are allowed to order them at their own discretion (although there were, in the latter country, some rules if these were ordered on the public health system).

So how does the UK rate internationally in numbers of MRI scanners? Japan is top of the list, with over fifty-five

MRI scanners per million people[90]. The USA, with over forty, is second, and Germany is third, with just under thirty-five. Australia and France have about fifteen, and as the normal table of developed countries runs out at Poland, which has only nine, you will be looking in vain for the UK's position on the list. In 2017, we had a grand total of just over six per million, roughly half the number of Slovenia. The bad news is that twenty-nine percent of these scanners were over ten years old and there was no plan to replace them[91].

What about hospital beds? While the overall number of beds is not in itself the sole determinant of a good healthcare system, it surely gives some idea of the capacity of a system, an important consideration if it were ever to be stress tested by a pandemic, to take a random example. Again, not good reading. The UK is miles down the list of OECD countries, at a total of 2.3 beds per 1,000 people[92]. This compares poorly with Germany (7.8 beds) and France (5.7 beds). The UK numbers are not dramatically different from those of the USA and Canada but the NHS still lags behind nevertheless.

Of course, not all hospital beds are created equal. ITU bed capacity became a much-quoted statistic in the pandemic, both as a warning for future pandemics, and a way to scaremonger the public into complying with lockdowns. Indeed, at times our very freedoms and civil liberties appeared to be dictated by our ITU capacity.

Again, the UK is disappearing in the rear-view mirror compared to many other countries, and the NHS does not seem to have done much to change this since the pandemic. According to figures from 2023, the much-derided USA is way ahead of its competitors, with 34.7 intensive care beds per 100,000 of the population[93]. Germany also does extremely well, with over 29 intensive care beds; indeed, the relatively low COVID death rate in Germany was partly put down to their excellent capacity. The UK comes in way, way, way down the list at 6.6 beds per 100,000 people, approximately half the number in Italy and France. What was that again about being the envy of the world?

Of course, hospital beds in themselves are of no use: there must be trained staff on the wards. One of the UK's superficially impressive responses to COVID was the setting up of 'Nightingale' wards, to provide extra capacity for patients on ventilators. But problems naturally occurred when it became clear there were not enough trained NHS personnel to staff them properly.

Let us look at doctors and nursing staff separately. The list of doctors per thousand head of population is headed by Austria, with 5.35. The UK, meanwhile, trails behind in twentieth place, with 3.03, way behind Germany, Australia, and Italy[94]. We are slightly higher on the nursing rankings, but with only 8.2 we are well behind Australia and Germany, who have around twelve, and Switzerland and Norway, who top the list with almost eighteen[95]. Interestingly, Singapore has less doctors and nurses than the UK by head of population, at 2.7 and 7.6 per 1,000 respectively[96], yet still blows us away on outcomes.

Another important parameter, one that flows directly from capacity, is that hardy old perennial, *waiting lists*. In the UK, long waiting lists feature prominently in the media, causing misery and despair to those who read the papers, let alone those stuck in the system. We know the backlog generated by COVID in the UK has been horrendous in the years since[97], but how do our waiting times compare to those in other countries? By this metric, you may well have expected the UK to do particularly badly, but in fact, in this area, the NHS is pretty much in the middle of the pack. The UK fares much worse than Italy, but is surprisingly just ahead of Australia[98]. At this point, as we sift through the statistics, we must be grateful for small mercies and even a middling score can feel like a triumph.

What about equity? Treating everyone the same is supposed to be one of the great moral strengths of the NHS. We can return to the Commonwealth Fund which strains every sinew of its muscles to demonstrate the shortcomings of the US system. Their league table is especially instructive. Of the eleven healthcare systems ranked, the UK comes fourth in terms of equity[99]. Only fourth? Yes, behind Australia, Germany, and Switzerland (even to the casual observer, it should be becoming obvious that Australia and Germany are clearly doing something right). In terms of healthcare outcomes, however, even the sympathetic Commonwealth Fund leaves us in ninth place (Australia came first, in case you were wondering). Somehow, it seems that equity and access to care do not lead to the best outcomes; or at least they do in Australia, but not in the UK.

As referred to *passim*, the COVID pandemic provided something of a stress test for various healthcare systems across the world. Direct comparisons are again problematic, due to geographic isolation and different political cultures, which enabled some areas to carry out much more draconian border controls. There is also the thorny issue of how COVID deaths were recorded. On this last point, the UK was much less strict than other countries, and sometimes rather *too* honest, so that at points in the viral new cycles, the UK appeared something of a plague island, bursting at the seams with dangerous new variants, and thousands of deaths a day.

It is not hard to attribute much of this to the NHS itself, although the extent to which the NHS is politicised and state-run does leave it particularly vulnerable to poor decisions by weak or ignorant politicians. One of the more accurate comparisons can be found in the *Lancet*, and here we refer to one specific variable, the reported mortality rate due to COVID per 100,000[100]. Here the UK is at just over 130 deaths, very similar to the USA. For Western Europe, the average mortality rate is 94.7, so we are not doing great in terms of raw figures. France had 97.4 and Germany 66.4. Remarkably low rates were seen in Australia (4.7) and Singapore (7.4). The former because it shut itself off from the rest of the world, and the latter because it knew what it was doing.

Expected life expectancy at birth is another tricky metric to judge. It has been estimated that only twenty percent of life expectancy in the developed world is due to available healthcare, and instead is mainly determined by wealth, diet, exercise, and lifestyle. It is not easy to adjust for a Mediterranean diet in the statistics, for example, or eating too much fructose corn syrup or quarter-pound cheeseburgers. Developed countries' mortality rates are so bunched up together that conclusions cannot be drawn with confidence.

But again, the UK does not do especially well, with a life expectancy at birth of just under 82 for both sexes, putting us twenty-ninth out of 183 countries for which statistics exist. For once, we are only slightly behind Germany, but quite a bit behind Australia (84) in eighth place, and Singapore (just over 84) which comes in fifth place[101].

Another important statistic does not measure quality of healthcare itself, but public perception of healthcare. Good healthcare will generally correlate well with public satisfaction. We might assume the NHS to garner more public satisfaction that it really deserves (see delusion, NHS), but even here we are not pulling up any trees. The Gallup world poll database provides figures for both 2010 and 2020, to enable us to chart the change over time. In the UK, public satisfaction with the healthcare service dropped from eighty-eight percent to seventy-five percent (and has dropped much further since). Interestingly, public satisfaction in the US and Australia *rose* during the decade, so they are both now on eighty-three percent. So much for Americans hating their healthcare system, as the left would have you believe[102].

Looked at in isolation, we see more evidence of the cognitive dissonance inspired by our NHS. For example, the Kings Fund found in 2022 that:

'The latest British Social Attitudes (BSA) survey reveals that public satisfaction with the NHS fell by 17 percentage points between 2020 and 2021. Overall satisfaction with the NHS is now at 36 percent, down 17 percentage points from 2020, the lowest level recorded since 1997 and the largest year-on-year drop in the history of the BSA survey. This dramatic fall in satisfaction is mirrored across all NHS services – from inpatients and outpatients to accident and emergency, as well as general practice and dentistry – and across nearly all demographic groups.'

On the very same website, the following was also noted:

'Although these survey results seem very gloomy for the NHS, the public's faith in the core principles of the service does not appear to have been eroded. The overwhelming majority of respondents in 2021 agreed that the founding principles of the NHS 'definitely' or 'probably' apply: that the NHS should be free of charge when needed (94 percent), that the NHS should primarily be funded through taxes (86 percent) and that care should be available to everyone (84 percent). It would seem that the public do not want a radical overhaul of the NHS, rather a health service that is appropriately funded and staffed to deliver the quality of care they need.'[103]

It is also doubtful most of those questions were asked in an open way, with the insinuation that the 'founding principles of the NHS' are unique to the UK.

The statement that eighty-six percent of people think the NHS should be funded primarily through taxes is interesting, as it would not, in principle, rule out a form of state insurance. Nevertheless, these numbers are very high and do not tally with satisfaction levels regarding personal experience. The discrepancy does, however, illustrate what a hurdle politicians must tackle when it comes to public appetite for real change.

I would be interested to hear the response to the following: *'What if a radical overhaul of the NHS is needed to provide a health service that is appropriately funded and staffed, and to deliver the quality of care we all need?'*

Governments of all stripes have increased spending on the

NHS *in real terms* in recent decades. Labour dramatically increased spending during its time in office as 'New Labour' (1997-2010), and the Conservative/LibDem coalition increased spending much more slowly thereafter. However, the bold statistics do not tell the full story. The credit crunch and financial crisis created a huge public deficit and revealed a country living beyond its means. The country's excessive borrowing led to some inevitable belt tightening after New Labour's time in office, but it cannot be stated enough that spending continued to rise in real terms, even if less than previously.

Let us now explore thoroughly claims that the NHS is underfunded. For such claims to be true, we need to demonstrate that the UK spends less on healthcare than comparative countries. This could go some way towards explaining the UK's poor performance. It is important to note, at this stage, that simply spending more money is not always linked with better outcomes; if it were, the US, with its huge health expenditure, would have the best outcomes in the world, and Singapore, with its low spending, would have the among the worst. In fact, the situation is the opposite.

The results show that in the decade before the pandemic the UK did indeed spend less on healthcare than some other European countries, such as France or Germany[104]. That said, Spain and Italy spent less than the UK and have better outcomes across the board.

Outside Europe, the United States is the highest spender amongst developed countries in terms of spending on healthcare as a percentage of GDP, at almost seventeen percent (again, this is pre-pandemic). In Europe, the highest spender was Germany, at 11.7%, although it should be noted that Germany has an older population. France spent 11.06%. And the UK? Surprisingly, the figure was 10.15%. Remember, however, that this was pre-pandemic, so the gap has narrowed since, as the UK saw the biggest increase in healthcare spending of all the major countries of Europe. Now let us look at our favourite two test countries, Singapore and Australia. The figure for Australia spends is 9.91%, less than the UK, and yet Australia performs much better[105]. Singapore, meanwhile, spent just 4.08%.

Surely, we should be looking at countries that spend less but achieve more, and trying to see what we can learn from them, rather than increasing our healthcare spending willy-nilly to catch up with others in Europe. Domestic healthcare spending has soared since the pandemic, and the UK now spends similar amounts to the very highest spenders in Europe. Will this lead to the UK rapidly becoming just as good as the other countries, in terms of number of doctors, nurses, beds, MRI scanners, and the like, all while pursuing the same NHS model? Such at outlook seems, at best, wildly optimistic.

Most of what we have discussed is only relevant in terms of outcomes. It does not matter how many doctors or beds you have if the treatments are poor and everyone dies. How does the NHS compare in terms of outcomes when looking at the main causes of death? Comparisons with developing countries are not relevant here, as the major killers have a completely different profile, often being infectious diseases that spread due to poor sanitation or lack of immunisation. It sounds counter-intuitive, but high death rates of certain types of cancer in your population can indicate a healthier population, as people are living long enough to develop these conditions.

Five of the most common non-infectious causes of death in the UK are: ischaemic heart disease (number one in men), dementia (number one in women), lung cancer, strokes, and chronic lower respiratory disease, of which the most common type is COPD[106].

The death rate from cardiovascular disease per 100,000 people in the UK is 132, far worse than Australia (108.13) or Singapore (93.68). Italy and France also performed better[107]. To those who point out that this is due to our less healthy lifestyle, I would ask: is the job of the National Health Service not also one of prevention, i.e. upholding the aim of keeping us healthier in the first place?

We do not set the world alight on stroke mortality, either: the death rate per 100,000 in the UK is 34.5. In Singapore, it is 22.1, in Australia 26.2. In France, the figure is 24.5 and in Germany 31. Using the same metric, what are the numbers for Alzheimer's and other forms of dementia? The UK's death rate is 20.77. Interestingly all the other countries we have discussed have very similar rates, with Germany doing only slightly better. This may also be put down to the lack of suitable treatments options available, a situation that results in there being minimal differences. When it comes to chronic respiratory diseases, we have another poor performance in death rates. The UK (36.5), is way behind Singapore (10.6), and Australia (24.2). Germany (20.8) and France (12.7) also do far better than the UK.

As for cancers, this is tricky as there are so many types. Of breast cancer five-year survival rates for the big countries, the US was best at over eighty-eight percent[108]. Australia, France, and Germany were all over eighty-five percent. The UK was on eighty-one percent, in thirtieth place, just above China and Slovenia. Lung cancer five-year survival was also poor by comparison: the UK figure was 9.6%, which is half that of the USA. Our position on the table was level with India and just ahead of Columbia.

This is all a bit depressing, isn't it? And we have not even touched on mental health, an area that is one of the NHS's weak points.

In the UK, we generally have access to a free internet, so most of this information is out there in the public domain. The areas I have discussed as points of comparison for the NHS versus other countries were not chosen deliberately to put the NHS down. There was no cherry-picking, and indeed a certain patriotic streak in me would *like* the UK's performance to be outstanding. But it is impossible to look at these statistics and feel any sense of pride. I fully expected the NHS to come out somewhere in the middle. But we are beaten again and again by similar countries whose systems are on similar levels of funding.

Anyone is of course welcome do their own research and come to a different conclusion. But based on statistics, it is extremely difficult to make the case that the NHS is the best health system in the world, and to try and suggest that it would be if it was better funded ignores health systems that outperform it on less money, such as Australia, Singapore, and Italy.

Another person's research would, at best, result in a mixed bag of statistics showing that the NHS is, to put it kindly, pretty average. It is up to those who suggest more money is the answer to explain exactly where and how such extra money would be spent, and how it would achieve better outcomes.

It is easy sophistry for those who support a socialist model of healthcare to pick on the (rare) evidence of high ranking and good performance, and dismiss any bad statistics as being due to underfunding.

The oft-repeated statement that the NHS is the envy of the world does not survive beyond Dover (or Enniskillen for that matter).

.

13. A TALE OF TWO BABIES
Singapore vs London

When you become a father, you remember the little details, the tiny fingers wrapping around your own, the first time you see the baby's wrinkly face, the piercing noise of the first cry. You may forget the less fun bits, such as pacing around the hospital building in the pre-dawn darkness under yellow street lighting, eating dodgy hospital canteen food or unsatisfying instant noodles, the feeling of utter exhaustion, the ineffectual reassurance given to your partner, her forehead bathed in sweat as she sucks greedily at the nitrous oxide.

I remember the good and bad aspects of the births of both of my children, one born abroad, the latter born in the UK. I recall the good medical care and decent staff in both Singapore and London.

There, however, the similarities end.

Two babies, with the same parents. A six-year gap. Two different cities with two *very* different healthcare systems. The same destination, but different journeys.

We will begin with the story of the second pregnancy and birth. During a mild December in London, we had our first contact with the antenatal department at the local NHS hospital.

The first appointment was complicated by my wife needing

a minor procedure in the same department, thus necessitating a closer examination by a specialist. The nurse who performed the initial test booked an appointment for us to attend the outpatients' 'suite' at the hospital, situated next to the antenatal clinic.

We soon received a letter replete with the NHS logo at the top. Previously, hospitals printed their own crests at the top of letters, but this practice was dispensed with years ago, replaced by the little blue *NHS* lozenge in the name of uniformity. The letter gave the time, date, and location of our allotted appointment. The date was not suitable, and I also knew that the procedure may well be delayed due to my wife's unexpected pregnancy (as is normal practice). The letter gave a number to ring should the appointment not be convenient. As I am the medical professional in the family, my wife wanted me to be the one to call the number and rearrange the appointment.

'Thank you for calling the gynaecology department. Our staff are all busy dealing with other callers, you are number eighteen in the queue.'

Eighteen? Do not panic, stay calm. A whole bank of staff could be answering the phones. The queue might be shorter than expected. After holding for about twenty minutes, however, I was still only sixteenth in the queue. In the end, I gave up and called again later. Hopeless. Two further calls on subsequent days were equally futile.

To hell with the phone, I thought, the hospital was only a couple of tube stops from work, I could nip in on the way home and change the appointment in person. I found my way to the gynaecology department and approached the front desk. There was a medium-sized queue. Eventually, it was my turn for the shaven-headed, heavily-tattooed male receptionist to 'serve' me.

'You have to ring the appointments line,' he grunted.

'Yes, I've tried that, but the queue was too long.'

'I can't rearrange appointments from here,' he said, waving a well-chewed ballpoint pen. 'I can make a new appointment but it could be at least three months.'

Not much good, especially as my wife was nervous about her procedure.

Following these failed attempts, and my subsequent considerable efforts to rearrange my working week, we were able to make our initial out-patient appointment at the clinic. Naturally, though, as soon as the nurse discovered my wife was pregnant, the procedure was rearranged for the second trimester of the pregnancy. A predictable waste of everyone's time.

As for the antenatal clinic itself, this appointment was booked by a self-referral online. After a couple of weeks, the appointment came through for the 'booking visit'. This is normally the first visit to the antenatal department in your chosen hospital. The visit consists of two parts. Firstly, there is the dating scan (which then dates the pregnancy, rather than relying solely on the last normal menstrual period or LNMP), and secondly, there is a chat with the midwife, who takes a full medical and obstetric history, while also arranging all the necessary blood tests, such as screening tests for chromosomal disorders, infectious diseases, blood type, and the like.

I assumed the midwife appointment and scan would be on the same day, but they were in fact split into two appointments, with the scan taking place on the Friday before Christmas Eve and the midwife booking visit taking place the day after Boxing Day. The first date was doable for us, but the second one was a pain. We were due to spend Christmas with my family and would have had to cut our visit short.

Frustration. Yet again there was a number to ring, and yet again I was in a queue, beginning as the *nineteenth* caller, this time. Determined to preserve my holiday, I stayed on the line as long as possible. After almost ninety minutes, however, having reached number six in the queue, I could bear it no longer and hung up, my nerves shredded by crackly muzak versions of *Nessun Dorma*, or Rick Astley's *Never Gonna Give You Up* on a very short loop, probably chosen deliberately to force you into hanging up (or hanging yourself) in despair. Jesus wept. I rebooked all our (non-refundable) return train journeys and rang my parents to cut short our holiday.

The scan appointment went smoothly enough. The result was normal and the radiographer was very professional. There was only an hour of waiting, which is pretty good by NHS standards. Of course, the immense pleasure prospective parents feel when viewing the first scan is always tempered by the dread of something going wrong. Having worked in Obstetrics and Gynaecology, I knew this was more common that people imagined. A bit nervous, I went for a pee in the male toilets, situated a great distance from the antenatal clinic. The toilets looked as though they had not seen a mop for months. I thought: shouldn't hospital loos be *cleaner* than average? I've seen pub toilets on a Friday night in better states.

Our second midwife appointment (our third visit to the hospital) took place, as planned, just after Christmas. The snag was my wife's DVT (deep vein thrombosis), a condition she developed ten years ago after a long-haul flight. The midwife wanted a doctor's opinion. Fair enough, I thought, watching as the midwife phoned an obstetrician or haematologist for an opinion regarding DVT prophylaxis. Rather than getting a prompt opinion, however, we were booked into yet *another* clinic to see the obstetricians. Our hearts sank. When would this take place? In two weeks' time.

After a typically stressful London bus ride home, we found an envelope on our welcome mat: the NHS letter regarding my wife's second, rearranged, appointment for her procedure, which would take place the following week. So, after three hospital visits in two and a half weeks, we had to visit the wretched place twice more in the next few days, attending two clinics that took place in rooms that were, literally, next to each other. Pretty understandably, my wife burst into tears.

The second out-patient visit was with the same nurse.

'Consultants normally do these procedures if you're pregnant, so we won't be able to do it today. I'll book you in for next week.'

Well, *bloody hell*. Tongue biting and wringing of hands. I felt like offering to do the sodding procedure myself. There was one mild silver lining, though: the third appointment was the same day as the upcoming obstetric visit, so I only needed to take one day off work.

The consultant was present at the clinic on this occasion and carried out the colposcopy, which was normal.

'The initial test was essentially normal, so you didn't really need to come, you could have come after you'd given birth.'

Not exactly what we wanted to hear, but we were at least reassured that everything was fine.

At the obstetric appointment later that day we saw a senior house officer who knew less than I did about anticoagulation in pregnancy. She called in the registrar, who, although very friendly, did not know much, either. We were therefore booked in for the *seventh* appointment of this seemingly endless farce, one week later, to see the medical obstetric consultant. He was, in fairness, highly competent and gave excellent advice.

The ridiculous thing about this experience is that nothing was medically wrong. The radiographer who performed our twelve week scan was excellent. The midwife was very good, and the medical obstetrician was faultless. But if this administrative mess can result from a normal pregnancy and a (virtually) normal test, I dread to think what would have happened if something had been abnormal.

Seven appointments took place, when three (at the absolute most) would have been enough. What a waste of effort, money, and time. The doctors, midwife, nurses, and radiographers performed very well; the inflexible, inefficient *system* did not. And the system we are taking about, for better or worse, is the NHS. The number of appointments, the time spent on the phone, the difficulty accessing specialists and the poor level of cleanliness (in the toilets at least) did not bode well for the ordeal to come.

Our experience in Singapore a few years earlier was utterly different. As expatriates with insurance provided in our package, we went private. Ah, you might say, the first alarm bells ringing, *you* can afford it, while others might not be able to. Ability to pay should not be the sole determinant of good health care. Yet it turns out that antenatal and obstetric care need not be so expensive after all, especially when you realise how much an average family in the UK pays into the NHS every year via taxation.

Our GP referred us to a female consultant gynaecologist at Mount Elizabeth Hospital in Singapore, one of the Parkway group of private hospitals. Our first antenatal appointment, for twelve-week blood tests and checks, took place at the adjacent Mount Elizabeth Medical Centre. The clinic was surprisingly small, although smart and clean inside. The lifts were likewise very cramped.

My wife underwent her routine tests as we waited for our appointment. Only five minutes later, we were shown into another tiny room, containing a tiny desk, behind which sat our tiny obstetrician.

Dr Serena, a Chinese Singaporean, introduced herself, took a history, and carried out a quick examination. The ultrasound equipment, with monitor, was attached to the end of the bed, and Dr Serena carried out the scan herself, describing all the body parts as they appeared on the screen: the head, the spine, the leg, and the little heartbeat. As this was our first child, it was an intense and private moment, tears springing all too readily. A couple of buttons were then pushed, we heard a whirring noise, and soon received two Polaroid-like pictures to prove that we were indeed 'expectant'.

Unless there is a medical reason to do more, the NHS provides two ultrasound scans. Whilst the twelve-week scan is a brief 'dating scan' that ascertains how far along the mother is, the twenty-week scan is far more detailed. The little embryo, with a primitive nervous and circulatory system, is now a foetus, big enough to tell the sex and also to see if there are any anatomical problems.

On the NHS, if your twenty-week scan is normal, the next time you see your baby will be when he or she is delivered into the world in that extraordinary, complex and bizarre phenomenon known as human birth.

In Singapore, however, a scan takes place again at sixteen weeks, then twenty weeks, and then every four weeks until thirty-six weeks, after which the scans take place weekly. At each visit, the consultant carries out the checks, repeats the scans, and discusses your progress. And so, we went up the small lift with the brown and cream wallpaper to the small consulting rooms and saw the same small consultant all the way through the pregnancy.

On the NHS, my wife did have a couple of midwife checks at an antenatal centre attached to a minor-injuries unit near our home. These visits involved long waiting times and were notable for their relative lack of continuity, as she saw a different midwife each time. This meant her fundal height (the size of her baby bump) was measured by different midwives, resulting in different readings. Twice she was sent for urgent scans as they thought the baby was not growing. On both occasions, the scans were normal. In Singapore the same person, using the same methodology, did the examination and the scan each time. There was no need for duplication, confusion, or stress.

My wife returned from her NHS midwife visits clutching a bunch of leaflets explaining what the blood tests meant, what the scans were for, and what she should expect in the pregnancy. All very well, but we received no leaflets in Singapore throughout any of our antenatal clinics. We did not need leaflets because we could simply ask the specialist, who answered all our questions.

After thirty-six weeks, my wife was back at the Mount Elizabeth Medical Centre to have a CTG, a trace of the baby's heartbeat. All the results were normal and reassuring. After the visit, we were given some forms, and told to go to the payment section of the Mount Elizabeth Hospital next door. Up to that point, the consultant had signed our claim forms after each visit, but for hospital pre-admission the procedure was different. We handed over a credit card and filled in a few forms before receiving a couple of documents to present to reception when the big day came.

This seemed a bit of hassle at the time, but the benefits became clear later on. When my wife started her contractions (amazingly, on the afternoon of the expected delivery date), we walked the two hundred metres to the hospital (another huge advantage of living in tiny Singapore) and handed our paperwork in at reception. Within five minutes, we were met by a smiling midwife who whisked us up to the delivery suite, even carrying my wife's overnight bag for her.

All the rooms were huge and single occupancy, with a healthy dad-sized sofa for hubby to get some kip. My wife changed into a gown and climbed into the delivery bed. An epidural was administered just after midnight, and Dr Serena popped in during the wee hours to see how dilated my wife was. An ARM (artificial rupture of membranes, or breaking the water) was then carried out, and we were left to get some sleep.

In the UK, my wife's waters broke in the early evening. We hailed a cab to the hospital, made our way to the pre-delivery admissions ward, and were examined by a nurse. My wife was not very dilated, so we were told to go home and wait until the contractions start. We did so, went back to bed and then, at three am, whoops, off went the contractions. Back to the hospital. Same room, same nurse or midwife (we weren't introduced).

'Not dilated enough, walk around the block a few times and go to the twenty-four-hour *Costa Coffee* on the ground floor.'

Right-ho. We did a couple of laps of the hospital and attempted a coffee, but by now my wife was doubled up in pain. Back up to the clinic for another attempt, still not very dilated. We were advised to go home and count the time between contractions. There was absolutely no way I could take my wife home in that amount of pain, so I asked if there were any beds available on the antenatal ward.

'There's only one left at the moment,' we were told reluctantly.

'Well, it'll have to be that one,' I said.

Without much enthusiasm (read none), we were admitted to the antenatal ward. It was still dark outside. We were shown to a six-bed bay. All the other beds were empty, so no sign of the almost full ward we heard about. At this point, the pain of the contractions was becoming unbearable. Nobody came to our bed, so after twenty minutes I approached the nurses' station to ask for some pain relief. Again, despite being perfectly polite, I encountered the same reluctance, even some sighing and 'yes, we'll get round to it, we are very busy entering details on the computer and writing up notes, don't you know.'

After ten more minutes, nothing had happened, so I literally grabbed a nurse and pointed to my wife, who was by this time in agony. This nurse (or midwife) arranged immediately for my wife's bed to be wheeled into the delivery suite, where we had a room of our own. A nice midwife took over, my wife was given gas (nitrous oxide), and a CTG was set up. This all happened *reasonably* quickly, over a thirty-minute period, but nobody was exactly rushing.

Dawn was breaking: sunlight had begun to poke through the gaps in the cheap yellowed blinds. Only then did I realise how stiflingly hot it was. But the window was impossible to open, so we were left sweating, as were the staff. A huge contrast to the gentle air conditioning of Mount Elizabeth Hospital.

Back to Singapore six years earlier. The CTG was set up in anticipation of the delivery. The time was now seven am, and the sun had appeared. The sun rises at the same time every day in Singapore, all year long, because it is bang on the equator. If it is still dark when you wake up, it means an almighty thunderstorm.

My wife's contractions increased in frequency and a midwife popped in to give her advice on how to push. At a quarter to eight, Dr Serena reappeared. Speedily, and with remarkably little fuss, she delivered our daughter. As she knew I was a doctor (I had referred several patients to her), she explained everything as she went along. I cut the cord, and the baby was weighed and cleaned. A paediatrician arrived and performed a full exam. My daughter was then expertly wrapped in a baby blanket and given to me. The baby blanket bore the words:

'A Miracle of Mount Elizabeth'

I held my daughter for a couple of wonderful minutes before handing her to my wife.

There was a large TV in the room. For the next hour or

so, my wife slept, as did the baby, while I watched a program about serial murderers. The catering staff brought in a full English breakfast for me and some noodles for my wife (I filled out a form for breakfast preferences when we completed the pre-admissions forms). I munched through bacon, egg, and toast, washed down with freshly squeezed orange juice and a pot of coffee, while texting friends and relatives the good news.

After an hour, we moved to the postnatal ward, where mother and baby were issued with matching electronic identity bracelets. Our window looked onto a view of pools and palm trees. The room was huge, akin to a decent sized hotel suite, with a private bathroom and a forty-inch plasma screen TV. A bunch of flowers sat on the table, pre-prepared by hospital staff, next to a large bowl of fruit. An incubator/baby cot had been set up.

Various packages were offered at the pre-admission check. Among the options were huge suites with extra bedrooms for family members, presumably for foreigners flying in to give birth in Singapore. As we lived round the corner, it did not feel necessary to do this, nor would it have been worth the extra cost. Instead, we chose a standard room. Our standard package included one night on the delivery suite, plus two more nights on the ward.

The nurses frequently took my new daughter off to the nursery, where small incubators were lined up containing tiny screeching babies. This enabled my wife to wash, rest and sleep without needing to look after the baby twenty-four hours a day. Over the next two days, we attended breastfeeding sessions, new mother chats on topics that included feeding, how to wrap your baby up, what to expect in the first few days, and nappy changing. By the time we were discharged, after two very relaxing nights, my wife felt full of confidence and knew exactly what to expect in the days ahead. Even with a GP as a husband, an extra layer of security had been applied.

We met Dr Serena again a few weeks later, thanked her, and gave her a card. She performed a post-natal check on my wife. And that was that.

Back in the NHS, several abnormal patterns on the CTG trace showed the babies' heart rate dropping during contractions and staying low a while too long. After five hours, the decision was made to proceed with a caesarean section. Being a doctor, I understood the terminology of the doctor's explanation and translated it for my wife. Imagine, though, a poor single mum on her own with no support, unable to follow anything.

We were lucky that the birth took place in the daytime. Colleagues warned me of the very high caesarean section rate and complications at this hospital, especially at night, when the junior doctors were expected to manage everything, and the consultants, though technically on call, 'never come in'.

Fortunately, a very experienced registrar and a consultant performed my wife's procedure. She was wheeled into the operating theatre next door, given an epidural, and a 'level two' emergency caesarean section was speedily performed. She lost over two litres of blood during the operation, which is a heck of a lot. After two minutes, we heard our son's cries for the first time. I cut the umbilical cord again and he was wrapped in a small blanket and handed to me.

Little sausage was checked by a paediatrician and off we went to the post-delivery bay, where my wife was found to have a low-grade fever. While I doubted this was anything serious, it meant another two full nights in hospital. The baby was not washed, 'we don't wash the new-borns', we were told, and we had to provide our own nappies and baby blanket.

That evening, my wife and new son were transferred to a bay of six mothers and babies. A gloomy place, not only hellishly hot, but with corridors and bays shrouded in darkness. There was no real privacy and no chance for my wife to get any decent sleep. The food was edible, though tasteless. The common toilet, twenty metres away, was always occupied. On one of the other beds, there lay a woman who constantly yelled into her mobile phone in Arabic, even at night, seemingly unconcerned by the effect this had on the other patients. Her newborn screeched the place down, filling the bay with dreadful noise. Next to my wife was a young mum, wailing and weeping bitterly with almost suicidal despair: Dad was nowhere to be seen.

My visits, bringing lots of sushi, other decent food, and magazines, didn't do much to raise my wife's spirits. Just as she was due to go home, the doctor was called away from his rounds due to an emergency. Too late to be discharged, she was forced to spend a third night in the hospital.

Apart from the blood loss and the semi-urgent c-section (hardly a rare occurrence), mother and baby were safe and well. Although tired and drained, post blood transfusion my wife was in good health. Slightly swollen ankles were the only outward evidence of a hospital stay. Her caesarean section scar healed well, and she began to breast feed with no problems. But did it *really* have to be such an awful experience overall? Did a happy occasion *need* to be so miserable? Couldn't the

NHS do the background stuff a bit better?

My Grandmother once told me that childbirth is the only time you go into hospital for a positive reason and a joyous experience. Yet I dread to think of the ordeal for first time mothers, single mums, those without medical professionals in the family, or, God forbid, those for whom things go wrong. It would be a gothic nightmare. And bear in mind this hospital was in one of the nicest parts of London, showing no apparent issues with recruitment and a full quota of nurses and midwifes in evidence.

This NHS hospital did have a private maternity unit, although the costs were similar to those found in a private hospital. Given our positive experience in Singapore, I did investigate the cost of having a baby privately in London. Most insurance companies do not cover childbirth, partly due to the high indemnity costs that obstetricians need to cover themselves, and because the NHS is so ubiquitous and free at the point of delivery.

The cheapest package we found cost just under ten thousand pounds, was for low-risk pregnancies only, and was midwife-led. A more typical cost was over fifteen thousand pounds, and would be even higher if a caesarean was needed. Private hospitals at the top of the pile charged far more. The high fees are justified, as enough rich people in London can afford to pay, and because the UK does not have a competitive marketplace for private medicine, there is no downward pressure on costs.

Another problem with private obstetric care in the UK is the lack of post-natal care for the baby. If the costs of having a baby privately are astronomical, the costs of an admission to paediatric intensive care, or PICU, would be far more. Even in Singapore, our insurance only covered my wife's care and a basic paediatric check on the baby. Had the baby needed intensive care, or a prolonged hospital stay, we would have been seriously out of pocket. This bit of small print luckily did not affect us, although it did affect some of my patients in Singapore, one of whom ended up with a bill of the equivalent of fifty thousand pounds.

Because Singapore has a much more open, competitive market for healthcare, costs for private maternity cover are pushed down, despite its excellent facilities rivalling the best in London. Partly due to this, insurance companies are far more likely to cover maternity. Our insurance was fairly cheap by international standards, the maternity option costing roughly the equivalent of seven hundred pounds per year, paid for as part of my job package.

When you add up the cost of the frequent antenatal visits, consultant led care, admissions, three nights in the suite, and the maternity care, the whole amount in Singapore came to about four thousand pounds, of which the insurance paid half. This meant we actually paid just over two thousand pounds, or closer to three thousand when you add the annual cost of the insurance itself.

You will possibly be thinking this is unaffordable to most people in the UK. But consider that average annual disposable household income in the UK is just over twenty-nine thousand pounds[109], possibly around thirty-eight thousand before tax. This household would pay over eight thousand pounds each in tax and national insurance, of which around nineteen percent goes to the NHS[110]. You could argue that our average household is paying around sixteen hundred pounds each a year into the NHS, a figure not too dissimilar to the amount my wife and I ended up paying in Singapore.

It is also true that, whilst you do not have babies every year of your life, you *do* pay taxes every year, meaning that money goes out regardless of whether you have babies or not. These are rough figures and have certain over-simplifications. The NHS is a training institution as well (another role it has acquired by stealth over the years), and the only way a doctor can be trained in the UK, so you must accept the consultants of tomorrow gaining experience in treating you, especially for more common procedures such as caesareans.

Notwithstanding the negatives in the NHS experience, the core medical care we received was excellent in both the UK and Singapore. Things could easily have been reversed, with a normal delivery in the NHS and a caesarean in Singapore, it was just the way things worked out. But the NHS experience seemed designed to make you feel miserable, depersonalised, and disempowered. And how glum for our imagined single mum to be discharged from the system and back to her London flat with a bunch of leaflets and no real support. To be already stressed and terrified, your life having been changed forever, and be trapped on an overheated ward with a grotty paint job, crummy food, a total lack of privacy, no toilet to yourself, and nobody with the time to come and sit with you and ask you if you are OK.

It is not the NHS that safely delivers your baby: the hard work of the doctors, nurses and midwives does that. But the monopoly of the NHS ensures that you will use it for childbirth, unless you are very well off. We can do better than this. Why was it such a pleasure to go through childbirth in a small city state on the equator, and such a misery in the world's first ever industrialised country? To think that this is only about the money is a delusion.

CONCLUSION

So, having gone thought all that, where are we now?

As we started the book with a defined delusion, or *delusions*, we can now offer a few facts in their place, one which now seem undisputable.

Firstly, let us respond to some of the earlier statements.

The NHS is not the best healthcare system in the world.

There is no evidence that the NHS is the most moral or civilised healthcare system in the world, and any such judgement must always be made against outcomes.

There is no evidence that the NHS would become the best healthcare system in the world, even if it did receive more funding.

A few more delusions can also be discounted using the following truths:

- **The NHS is not unique to the UK.**
- **The NHS is only one amongst many healthcare systems that provide care free at the point of**

- **delivery.**
- **Almost nobody in the developed world envies the NHS.**
- **The NHS is the not the only system funded primarily from taxation, although few other wealthy countries have a healthcare model as centralised as that of the UK.**
- **No comparable country in the world wants to copy the NHS model.**
- **Healthcare in other developed countries is frequently both free and equitable.**

There is much evidence that the above statements are true and their respective delusions are false. Only by retreating into an ideologically socialist mindset is it possible to ignore available evidence, both from lived experience and from statistical outcomes.

Ideology is a poor basis on which to anchor a healthcare system, as it does not often survive contact with the real world. This can apply equally to ideology on the right: full exposure to market forces would be as unpalatable as socialist planning.

Real change to the NHS is probably further away than ever. The COVID pandemic should have severely knocked confidence and satisfaction with the NHS, and recent surveys do show a marked drop in the public's approval[111], mainly due to negative press publicity and real-world experience, such as horrendous waiting times for ambulances or in A&E.

The backlog will take years to clear. Mental health has been neglected, especially amongst children. Cancers delayed in their presentation now require more radical and costly treatment than would have been necessary. In the winter of 2022/23, ambulance waits for heart attacks and strokes exceeded ninety minutes[112]. This is not the mark of a civilised country. If you can order a pizza and have it delivered to your home within thirty minutes, why can you not get an ambulance in that space of time?

Picasso become a great painter before he became an innovative cubist. He got the basics right first, before pursuing the radical stuff. The great All-Blacks rugby teams, and dominant Australian cricket teams, often left others scratching their heads, trying to work out the reason for their success. It isn't rocket science: they work their backsides off in order to get the basics right again and again and again. The basics of days to day healthcare is the area in which the NHS needs to do so much better, before we even start talking about tertiary care and hyper-specialisation.

The pandemic, with its clapping for heroes and eulogising of the NHS by all major political parties, was one long propaganda piece for the service, to the detriment of public debate. Public discourse regarding several issues in the political sphere, but particularly healthcare provision, has drifted leftward in the UK over the last decade, a process that began even before COVID. This despite (or maybe because of) the Conservatives being in power for much of that time.

Far from replacing, or reforming the NHS, the debate is more likely to centre on increased funding and a doubling down on the same model. Gordon Brown, never a politician given to much self-doubt when it comes to spending public money, recently supported a proposal to enshrine the NHS in law, making any future changes to the system almost impossible and closing debate down for good[113].

If you have self-serving, short-termist, incompetent ministers (of any party) running the health service, you will soon enough have an NHS that is self-serving, short-termist and incompetent.

In a way that many people in Britain find hard to understand, directly paying money for healthcare exists across the globe, without any weird moral hangup. In most developed countries, if you strain your wrist playing tennis, you go and pay for a physiotherapist. You would not call your NHS (or equivalent) GP, demand a referral, and then complain about the wait, when you are perfectly able to afford direct private treatment. You are not paying to jump the queue: you are paying for up front healthcare, and you will find the physiotherapist who treats you will not be a money-grabbing evil capitalist but a caring professional. Rather like physios in the NHS in fact, if they have not all left for Australia, Canada, and New Zealand by now.

The current leader of the Labour Party at the time of writing, abetted by his Shadow Health spokesman, has even pledged that Labour would seek to *nationalise* general practice and take all GP surgeries back into centralised NHS control[114]. This would mean that the one part of the NHS that is locally run and managed by doctors, as on the continent, would be put under state control, to be run by managers and bureaucrats. God help us. Such an ill-considered move would deplete the workforce hugely, as most partners over fifty-five would retire, recruitment would become much more difficult, and continuity of care, already badly stretched and undermined by overwhelming demand, would come to a complete halt.

Most staff in primary care go above and beyond, but if you treat GPs like employees with set hours and set tasks, the goodwill will dry up and doctors will simply clock in and clock out. If you start paying people only for what they do, they will, soon enough, only do what you pay them for.

As I write, there are planned strikes over pay by unions representing nurses, paramedics, junior doctors and even consultants. But why should their pay demands have anything to do with central government? And aren't there moral duty or care issues around health workers striking? Surely threatening strike action is no way to conduct negotiations, when innocent patients are poised to suffer through no fault of their own.

Those who scream out about the two-tier system fail to realise that we already have one. Between seven and eleven percent of the public go private, a similar proportion to the number who go to public schools. The proportion being so small is what makes private medicine so elitist. If, say, fifty percent of the public could access private healthcare, would that not represent a better two-tier system, given that tiers are inevitable under any health system? Would that not be better that the present situation, in which only a small number can take advantage in this way? Ability to jump the queue by paying will always exist, unless you really want communism, but even then, complete equity would only exist in theory. All healthcare systems are created equal, but some are more equal than others.

The original idea of providing all citizens with a welfare safety net has been lost in the wind. The welfare state, and most especially the NHS, is now seen as a universal entitlement, whether one can afford alternative cover or not. These days, spending on healthcare is not only seen as virtuous, but also as a 'government' expenditure, rather than the money coming from the taxpayer, thus leaving no incentive to reduce demand.

When it comes to the NHS, and, more worryingly, society in general, tax cuts are now considered almost evil, even by the bulk of the Tory party, whereas increased public spending, especially on health, is considered automatically compassionate. This is something of a bizarre situation and would be interesting to test at the ballot box: if one party were to advocate overhauling the NHS, creating a large independent healthcare sector, and slashing taxes, who knows what the outcome would be. Yes, that party would be harmed, given the 'NHS delusion', but I do not think such proposals would be as unpopular as some on the left think, hence why they immediately demonise and resort to scaremongering when they perceive that the NHS is under threat.

Whilst the workforce crisis in the NHS is bad enough, in the care sector, things are even worse. Social care is even more disproportionally affected by our ageing population and the staffing numbers are so bad it does not bear thinking about. It cannot be the case that too many of our own citizens are either too lazy or too uncaring to work in care jobs that support the elderly. It is more likely that they are penalised by a perverse tax system that makes it easier to stay at home on benefits.

The future is likely bleak, and there are four potential scenarios that may pan out in the years ahead. The first is that the current model of NHS funding remains untouched, with some petty nationalisations, as mentioned above. The NHS will not be seriously reformed, but will continue to swallow up ever larger sums of taxpayers' money, to the detriment of other public services such as schools, the police and defence. This would be funded by further borrowing or tax increases, which are already at record levels, further damaging the economy and the private sector (that pays for the NHS in the first place). Long waiting lists would become a permanent fixture. Waits in A&E to see a doctor would remain high, and, increasingly, waits for conditions such cancer would contribute to poor outcomes when compared to our European neighbours. High taxes and poor working conditions would lead to an even greater outflow of nursing and medical staff than there is now. This would seem to be the most likely outcome under a future Labour Government (or SNP in Scotland).

The second scenario is the unintentional (or otherwise) degradation of the current service. This involves no serious reform, but a much tighter hold on the national purse strings, with taxes and borrowing not being increased hugely. The NHS would be more affordable, but its inefficiencies would result in far fewer services being available. There would be reduced NHS access to IVF, podiatry, physiotherapy, minor surgery, and counselling, to name a few. These would eventually disappear from the NHS provision, being decommissioned as they had been deemed non-essential and too expensive. This would not happen overnight, but by a thousand decommissioning cuts. Out of desperation, far more people would go private, but most of them would be self-paying due to their inability to pay for insurance. This is pretty much what is happening today: I have seen much of it with my own eyes. Primary care itself may become more rarified, similar to NHS dentistry. This seems to be the most likely outcome under a continuing Conservative

Government.

A third possibility exists, and this is where things get a little more interesting. By an act of political courage, or (more likely) political necessity, due to the public's patience snapping, an 'honest conversation' takes place with the public to win hearts and minds. A complete overhaul of the system is unlikely, but the NHS becomes more streamlined as a *deliberate* act of policy, with some services no longer being covered, similar to the second outcome above, but as a planned focusing of the service, rather than healthcare provision simply falling to bits. Tax breaks and incentives are introduced to help people go private; the insurance sector is expanded to create genuine competition and keep prices down; the number of people needing to self-pay is reduced; and those with private insurance begin to constitute a much larger chunk of the population, say a quarter, while still relying on the NHS for their core needs. This would shift us somewhat towards the models in France and Germany. No political party in the UK supports this approach, although the Thatcher government would have been the nearest in recent memory to consider it.

The fourth possibility is a deliberate effort by the government of the day to create circumstances in which a large independent sector could thrive, resulting in up to half the population being covered by private health insurance, while those who could not afford private health insurance, or chose not avail themselves of it, would be covered by state health insurance. Like 'Obamacare', state insurance cannot take preexisting conditions into account. The NHS remains, but as a backup and guarantor of healthcare rather than in its current, all-pervasive form. The healthcare sector remains free at the point of delivery based on clinical need for all who chose to use it. This would bring the UK much nearer to the Australian system. Although a few doctors and a few political journalists would welcome this scenario, it is an approach that has never been the policy of any major political party in the UK.

I would have included further options, such as the UK adopting the Singaporean or American systems, but these two systems have only a vanishingly small chance of ever being adopted. Public entitlement and lack of self-reliance in the UK mean that the Singaporean system would be a non-starter. The US system would also never take root in the UK, as it has its own inherent flaws, and has been so demonised that implementing it would be politically impossible.

Ignoring the odds for the next UK general election, I regard the first option as having a seventy percent chance of coming true and the second as having over a twenty-five percent chance. The third option has maybe five percent chance at best, and the fourth certainly less than one percent.

Realistically, the pressure to overhaul the system can only come from the public. The political class is moribund and cowardly, preferring to chase opinion polls rather than provide real leadership. NHS workers display some militancy over pay, but public sector unions are more interested in their members' pay and pensions, rather than the existential state of the NHS, which they claim to support even as they put lives at risk by going on strike. Doctors, who could provide leadership on these points, have always been conservative with a small 'c', even when voting left, and are either too busy, too knackered, or too busy moving abroad to make a difference.

A bit of blue-sky thinking would help. Do doctors really

need to train at medical school for five years? Why not abolish 'bachelor of medicine and surgery' degrees completely? Why not have a three-year psychiatry degree, incorporating basic medical science if you want to become a psychiatrist? Junior doctor training would be much simpler. As long as there was a way to change your mind later, couldn't this be applied over the majority of medical specialities?

Regarding medical schools, couldn't they be independent and not for profit, possibly with some compulsory service in the NHS afterwards?

Shifting public opinion will drag politicians with it, and this is where we must place our hope for the future, despite the propaganda and misinformation from the mainstream media. The public's patience will, perhaps, eventually run out, and we will get either an NHS befitting a first-world country or a replacement service that fulfils this requirement.

One wonders just how bad things must get. How long do waiting lists have to be? How many people must die of cancer while waiting for treatment? How long do ambulance waits have to be? How bad does the workload for NHS staff need to become, until they have had enough and no longer want to paper over the cracks?

There is one particularly depressing story that appeared in the print media recently. It is one that has been told many times, and its familiarity makes the narrative even more depressing as a consequence. The story normally concerns a male patient, often in his sixties. Men are notoriously bad at going to the doctors anyway, but the story normally involves an unpleasant diagnosis and the patient suffering some NHS delay, either due to a delay in referral, or an endless waiting list for treatment.

While on a waiting list, the patient takes a turn for the worse, and dies. The relatives left behind often say almost exactly the same thing: '*He could have gone private and we begged him to, but all his life he believed in the NHS and didn't approve of trying to jump the queue.*'

This may be a noble sentiment, but is it worth losing your life over? For the nearest and dearest who remain, is this point of principle really justified? Think of the empty chair at the graduation ceremony, the absent father at the wedding or the absent grandad at Christmas. Is love for the NHS so important that you are willing to risk your life for it? Surely the answer *must* be no.

Despite evidence to the contrary and the examples listed throughout this book, public opinion may prove impossible to shift. The public's unshakeable belief that the current NHS is the best way to deliver healthcare may well endure.

But if the public and politicians really are determined to stick with the current system, a serious change must take place. Patients will have to lower their expectations, be careful not to take their frustrations out on frontline staff, and be accepting of ever-lengthening waits for treatment, delayed diagnoses, and poorer service due to inadequate staffing. Demand will have to be reduced to match supply. A dose of realism regarding what the NHS and other public services can achieve will be essential, otherwise we will end up simply going round in circles like getting nowhere, telling ourselves we are the best in the world.

Just because a person loves the NHS and its founding principles, and believes that it is the best system in the world, this does not make it any more likely to be true. Critics, at least, cannot be accused of wishful thinking. Successful countries adapt and adjust according to circumstance, and are not afraid to study how others do things better. That is why Japan and Singapore did so well in the last half of the twentieth century.

Funding and delivery of healthcare should not be left to the state, especially one as poorly run as ours. It is far too important. To maintain that the NHS is the best healthcare model in the world flies in the face of reality and common sense. It is the ultimate delusion.

And delusions, as we have seen, can be fatal.

AUTHOR'S NOTE
January 2025

This book was completed in early 2024, and events in the NHS and the UK have since outpaced the narrative. Yet, despite seismic political change, nothing has emerged to contradict the premise of this book. Indeed, almost all predictions concerning the NHS and British Politics have been proved correct. This is unfortunate. With any pessimistic prospectus, one should 'want to be wrong', but goodness, to be proved so right is both somewhat satisfying, and ultimately profoundly depressing at the same time.

In 2024 the Conservative government displayed remarkable political genius by turning a large majority into a landslide loss within less than five years. This has led to a Labour Government, which nobody could ever accuse of political genius.

Before the election, the new Prime Minister and Health Secretary were making encouraging noises regrading NHS reform, but these proved fissile, disintegrating immediately on contact with the real world. This was particularly disappointing in the case of the Health Secretary, who recently visited two of the countries discussed in detail in this book, Singapore, and Australia, to study their healthcare systems. He should have come back fizzing with ideas, but we have only inertia and hand-wringing. There is clearly no appetite for real, radical reform, only for more public spending and public sector pay rises, which will prove unsustainable. The tinkling of cans being kicked down the road can be heard all over Whitehall.

The new Chancellor plans to pay for the increase in NHS funding by increasing borrowing (God help us) and, amongst other things, hiking national insurance for employers, thereby hammering the private sector which pays for the NHS. If companies cannot hire due to labour costs, they will grow more slowly, or there will be fewer jobs and fewer individuals and companies to pay tax in the first place. If ever robbing Peter to pay Paul was an apt analogy, this is it.

There existed the possibility that, as with Nixon in China, only Labour could truly be trusted to reform an institution which it politicised and socialised in the 1940's and has weaponised ever since. They have proved themselves not only ideologically incapable of the reforms required, but in every department (not just Health) they demonstrate staggering incompetency at every turn.

This returns us to our title. Universal healthcare paid for, managed, budgeted, and directed by central government through general taxation will not provide the best health service in the world. It is a delusion.

Oh, and in another analogy from the book, perennial loser England Football Manager Gareth Southgate lost the finals of the 2024 European championships and was knighted for his efforts. Rewarded for serial failure. A perfect exemplar of modern Britian.

REFERENCES

PREFACE

1 Westminster Abbey (2023) *NHS celebrates 75th anniversary* [online] Available at: https://www.westminster-abbey.org/abbey-news/nhs-celebrates-75th-anniversary

INTRODUCTION

2 The King's Fund (2002) *The NHS budget and how it has changed* [online] https://www.kingsfund.org.uk/projects/nhs-in-a-nutshell/nhs-budget

3 The i Paper (2023) *Ukrainian refugees give up on crisis hit NHS and travel home to warzone for medical treatment* [online] https://inews.co.uk/news/ukrainian-refugees-nhs-crisis-travel-home-war-zone-treatment-2083233

4 Football Orbit (2022) *Top 10 highest paid managers at the FIFA World Cup* [online] https://www.footballorbit.com/highest-paid-managers-2022-fifa-world-cup/

5 The Independent (2022) *NHS founding principles not up for discussion* [online] https://www.independent.co.uk/news/uk/nhs-bbc-nicola-sturgeon-humza-yousaf-health-secretary-b2229616.html

6 Ashcroft, M. & Oakeshott, I. (2022) *Life Support: The State of the*

NHS in an age of pandemics (Biteback)

PART ONE: THE NHS

1. PROPAGANDA

7 Kay, A. (2017) *This is Going to Hurt* (Picador)

8 World Population Review (2023) *Infant mortality by country, 2023* [online] https://worldpopulationreview.com/country-rankings/infant-mortality-rate-by-country

9 The Telegraph (2023) *The NHS is in crisis – is it time you went private?* [online] https://www.telegraph.co.uk/money/consumer-affairs/more-people-use-private-health-insurance-worth-paying/

10 Gallup (2023) *Americans sour on US healthcare quality* [online] https://news.gallup.com/poll/468176/americans-sour-healthcare-quality.aspx

11 BBC News (2023) *NHS – public satisfaction with health service drops to record low* [online] https://www.bbc.com/news/health-65093449

12 Clarke, R. (2021) *Breathtaking* (Abacus)

13 El-Gingihy, Y. (2019) *How to dismantle the NHS in 10 easy steps* (Zero books)

14 Hunt, J. (2022) *Zero, eliminating deaths in a post-pandemic NHS* (Swift Press)

15 Ashcroft, M. & Oakeshott, I (2022) *Life Support: The State of the NHS in an age of pandemics* (Biteback)

2. CLAPPED OUT?

16 Nature (2020) *Special Report: The simulations driving the world's response to COVID-19* [online] https://www.nature.com/articles/d41586-020-01003-6

17 BBC (2020) *Matt Hancock on testing for care home staff and residents* [online] https://www.bbc.com/news/av/uk-politics-52725547

18 The Sun (2020) *TV historian David Starkey compares NHS coronavirus response to 'paedophilia in Catholic Church* [online] https://www.thesun.co.uk/news/11688984/david-starkey-nhs-catholic-church/

19 The Spectator (2021) *The censorious war on lockdown sceptics* [online] https://www.spectator.co.uk/article/the-censorious-war-on-lockdown-sceptics/

20 BBC News (2021) *Covid-19: 10-year jail time for travel lies defended* [online] https://www.bbc.com/news/uk-56007798

21 Cochrane (2023) *Statement on Physical interventions to interrupt or reduce the spread of respiratory viruses' review* [online] https://www.cochranelibrary.com/cdsr/doi/10.1002/14651858.CD006207.pub6/full

22 Reason (2022) *There is little evidence that mask mandates had an important impact during the omicron surge* [online] https://reason.com/2022/02/18/there-is-little-evidence-that-mask-mandates-had-an-important-impact-during-the-omicron-surge/

23 Sky News (2020) *Coronavirus: PPE shipment flown in from Turkey fails UK safety standards* [online] https://news.sky.com/story/coronavirus-ppe-shipment-flown-in-from-turkey-fails-uk-safety-standards-11984368

24 The Evening Standard (2020) *Medical fetish site says its giving scrubs to NHS hospital amid coronavirus* [online] https://www.

standard.co.uk/news/uk/coronavirus-medical-fetish-site-gives-scrubs-nhs-hospital-a4402506.html

25 Metro (2021) *Omicron variant symptoms extremely mild, says doctor who discovered it* [online] https://metro.co.uk/2021/11/28/omicron-variant-symptoms-extremely-mild-says-doctor-who-discovered-it-15677135/

26 Reuters (2021) *Omicron is very serious threat what we know is bad, UK Health Official* [online] https://www.reuters.com/world/uk/omicron-is-very-serious-threat-what-we-know-is-bad-uk-health-official-2021-12-15/

27 Appleby, J. & Hunter, D. (2010) *Should the NHS be ring-fenced?* [online] https://www.bmj.com/bmj/section-pdf/186071?path=/bmj/341/7769/Head_to_Head.full.pdf

28 UK Government Website (2020) *Prime Minister Boris Johnson's statement to the House on coronavirus* [online] https://www.gov.uk/government/speeches/prime-ministers-statement-to-the-house-on-covid-19-23-june-2020

29 Our World in Data (2021) *Emerging COVID-19 success story: Germany's strong enabling environment* [online] https://ourworldindata.org/covid-exemplar-germany

30 Eurostat (2020) *Healthcare expenditure across the EU: Eurostat; your key to European statistics* [online] https://ec.europa.eu/eurostat/statistics-explained/index.php?title=Healthcare_expenditure_statistics_-_overview

31 The Lancet (2020) *Reduced mortality in New Zealand during the COVID-19 Pandemic* [online] https://www.thelancet.com/journals/lancet/article/PIIS0140-6736(20)32647-7/fulltext

32 BBC News (2020) *Covid: Australian anti-lockdown suspect's arrest draws controversy* [online] https://www.bbc.com/news/

world-australia-54007824

33 Live Science (2020) *Why an Australian COVID-19 vaccine caused false-positive HIV tests* [online] https://www.livescience.com/australia-covid-19-vaccine-false-positive-hiv-tests.html

34 The Guardian (2021) *Do not touch that ball advice prompts anger and humour from all fans* [online] https://www.theguardian.com/sport/2021/jun/02/do-not-touch-that-ball-covid-advice-prompts-anger-and-humour-from-afl-fans

3. GENESIS

35 Cohen, S. (2020) *THE NHS: Britain's National Health Service 1948-2020* (Shire)

36 Bartholemew, J. (2004) *The Welfare State We're In* (Biteback)

37 The National Archives (1951) *Attlee's Britain 1945-51* [online] https://www.nationalarchives.gov.uk/education/resources/attlees-britain/beveridge-report/

38 IFS (2012) *70th anniversary of the Beveridge Report: Where now for welfare?* [online] https://ifs.org.uk/articles/70th-anniversary-beveridge-report-where-now-welfare

39 Wellcome Collection (2022) *Eugenics and the welfare state* [online] https://wellcomecollection.org/articles/YxW0VhEAACEAi6qc

40 Past Medical History (2016) *Aneurin Bevan and the birth of the NHS* [online] https://www.pastmedicalhistory.co.uk/aneurin-bevan-and-the-birth-of-the-nhs/

4. GUILTY PARTIES

41 YouTube ThatcheriteScot (1989) *First ever televised Prime Ministers Questions* [online] https://www.youtube.com/

watch?v=6CiNqfEJLsw

42 The Health Foundation (2015) *How funding for the NHS has changed over a rolling ten-year period* [online] https://www.health.org.uk/chart/chart-how-funding-for-the-nhs-in-the-uk-has-changed-over-a-rolling-ten-year-period

43 The Guardian (2015) *Weaponising of mass distraction: Tories and Labour face off over NHS* [online] https://www.theguardian.com/politics/2015/jan/28/nhs-weaponising-mass-distraction-david-cameron-ed-miliband

44 UK Government Website (2011) *Speech on the NHS* [online] https://www.gov.uk/government/speeches/speech-on-the-nhs

45 The King's Fund (2017) *General Election 2017: who will be most generous to the NHS* [online] https://www.kingsfund.org.uk/blog/2017/06/general-election-most-generous-nhs

46 BBC News Website (2022) *Public Satisfaction with NHS drops to 25-year low* [online] https://www.bbc.co.uk/news/health-60917585

47 The London Economic (2021) *Best Tweets as Matt Hancock was 'busy saving lives' during Cummings' evidence* [online] https://www.thelondoneconomic.com/news/best-tweets-as-matt-hancock-was-busy-saving-lives-during-cummings-evidence-271411/

5. STATE OF AFFAIRS

48 British Medical Journal (2022) *Pandemic has accelerated demand for private healthcare, report finds* [online] https://doi.org/10.1136/bmj.o566

49 Arcadia Care Journey (2020) *Social determinants of health: unaddressed variable accounting for 80% of health outcomes*

[online] https://carejourney.com/social-determinants-of-health/

50 UK Government Website (2017) *Health profile for England: 2021* [online] https://www.gov.uk/government/publications/health-profile-for-england/chapter-1-life-expectancy-and-healthy-life-expectancy

51 Tufts University (2015) *Public and Private Sector Contributions to the research and development or the most transformative drugs of the last 25 years* [online] https://f.hubspotusercontent10.net/hubfs/9468915/tuftscsdd_june2021/pdf/public+and+private+sector+contributions+to+the+research+%26+development+of+the+most+transformational+drugs+of+the+last+25+years+.pdf

6. PRIMARY COLOURS

52 The Telegraph (2022) *Just one in four GPs are working full time* [online] https://www.telegraph.co.uk/news/2022/07/28/just-one-four-gps-works-full-time-new-data-reveals/

53 The Telegraph (2023) *Surgeons carrying out operations just once a fortnight* [online] https://www.telegraph.co.uk/news/2023/04/28/surgeons-carrying-out-operations-once-fortnight-nhs-chaos/

54 The Telegraph (2022) *Almost 1.5 million patients lose their GP as hundreds of practices close* [online] https://www.telegraph.co.uk/news/2022/08/29/almost-15m-patients-lose-gp-hundreds-practices-close/

55 Nursing Times (2018) *Sharp spike in number of physical assaults on NHS staff* [online] https://www.nursingtimes.net/news/workforce/sharp-spike-in-number-of-physical-assaults-on-nhs-staff-17-04-2018/

56 Report from the Clinical Imaging Board (2017) *Magnetic Resonance Imaging (MRI) equipment, operations and planning in the NHS* [online] https://www.sor.org/getmedia/b192cc1f-dc23-4d01-b928-df6bde46cc73/Magnetic%20Resonance%20Imaging%20(MRI)%20Equipment,%20Operations%20and%20Planning%20in%20the%20NHS_13

7. OUT OF SIGHT...

57 Health and Safety Executive (2022) *HSE publishes annual work-related ill health and injury statistics for 2021/22* [online] https://www.hse.gov.uk/statistics/

58 Chemist 4 U (2023) *Anti-depressant statistics UK* [online] https://www.chemist-4-u.com/guides/mental-health/antidepressant-statistics-uk/

59 Journal of Psychological Medicine (2021) *The evidence for cognitive behavioural therapy in any condition, population or context: a meta-review of systematic reviews and panoramic meta-analysis* [online] https://www.cambridge.org/core/journals/psychological-medicine/article/evidence-for-cognitive-behavioural-therapy-in-any-condition-population-or-context-a-metareview-of-systematic-reviews-and-panoramic metaanalysis/3BE55E078F21F06CFF90FFAD1ACEA5E0

60 Mind Diagnostics (2022) *Understanding the history of ADHD and what we've learned so far* [online] https://www.mind-diagnostics.org/blog/adhd/understanding-the-history-of-adhd-and-what-weve-learned-so-far

61 CDC (2024) *Data and statistics about ADHD* [online] https://www.cdc.gov/adhd/data/?CDC_AAref_Val=https://www.cdc.gov/ncbddd/adhd/data.html

62 The Telegraph (2023) *Number of children on disability benefits jumps after surge in ADHD and Autism cases* [online] https://www.telegraph.co.uk/business/2023/08/23/number-children-disability-benefit-adhd-autism-cases-soar/?n=@

PART TWO: THE REST

8. SINGAPORE

63 Straits Times (2018) *Lee Kuan Yew lauded for critical role in China's reform and opening-up* [online] https://www.straitstimes.com/tags/lee-kuan-yew

64 World Health Organisation (2025) *Cancer screening* [online] https://www.who.int/cancer/prevention/diagnosis-screening/screening/en/

65 The Commonwealth Fund (2020) *International Healthcare Systems Profiles: Singapore* [online] https://www.commonwealthfund.org/international-health-policy-center/countries/singapore

66 World Bank (2023) *Mortality rate, infant (per 1,000 live births) – Singapore* [online] https://data.worldbank.org/indicator/SP.DYN.IMRT.IN?locations=SG

67 Clark, D. via Statista (2019) *Benefit expenditure in the United Kingdom 2002/03-2018/19* [online] https://www.statista.com/statistics/283954/total-welfare-benefits-united-kingdom-uk-government-spending/

9. AUSTRALIA

68 Statista Research Department (2022) *Share of population with general private health insurance Australia 2021 by*

state [online] https://www.statista.com/statistics/1049235/australia-share-of-insured-persons-with-general-health-cover-by-state/#:~:text=Published%20by%20Statista%20Research%20Department%2C%20Jul%2015%2C%202022,had%20private%20health%20insurance%20that%20covered%20general%20treatment.

69 RACGP (2021) *General Practice Health of the Nation* [online] https://www.racgp.org.au/education/imgs/health-of-the-nation-2021-the-shape-of-general-pra

10. ACROSS THE CHANNEL

70 Germany Visa (2025) *Health Insurance in Germany – The German Healthcare System* [online] https://visaguide.world/international-health-insurance/germany/

71 The Commonwealth Fund (2020) *International Healthcare System Profiles: Germany* [online] https://www.commonwealthfund.org/international-health-policy-center/countries/germany

72 OECD iLibrary (2021) Government at a Glance 2021 [online] https://www.oecd.org/en/publications/government-at-a-glance-2021_1c258f55-en.html

73 The Global Economy.com (2020) *Doctors per 1,000 people - Country rankings* [online] https://www.theglobaleconomy.com/rankings/doctors_per_1000_people/

74 Dialog Health in France (2019) *Why France? The French health and social care system is internationally recognized as providing one of the best services of public health in the world as the French live healthier and longer.* [online] https://infrance.dialog-health.com/france-has-the-best-healthcare-system-in-the-world

75 Wise (2017) *Healthcare in France: A guide to the French Healthcare*

System [online] https://wise.com/us/blog/healthcare-system-in-france

76 Health Management (2010) *The Healthcare System in France* [online] https://healthmanagement.org/c/imaging/issuearticle/the-healthcare-system-in-france

77 Expat in France (2021) *French Mutelle: why 95% of people have one* [online] https://expat-in-france.com/french-complementary-health-insurance/

78 Commonwealth Fund (2023) *Dutch Healthcare system tops patient ranking* [online] https://www.commonwealthfund.org/publications/newsletter-article/dutch-health-care-system-tops-patient-rankings

79 MDPI (2023) *Covid-19 and Public Health Spending; Effects on the Economic Sustainability of the Spanish Private Healthcare System* [online] https://www.mdpi.com/1660-4601/20/2/1585

80 OECD iLibrary (2024) *Health at a Glance: Europe 2024* [online] https://www.oecd.org/en/publications/health-at-a-glance-europe-2024_b3704e14-en.html

81 International Citizens Insurance (2025) *Italian Healthcare System* [online] https://www.internationalinsurance.com/health/systems/italy.php

11. ALL AROUND THE WORLD

82 CNBC make it (2018) *Here's the real reason health care costs so much more in the US* [online] https://www.cnbc.com/2018/03/22/the-real-reason-medical-care-costs-so-much-more-in-the-us.html

83 Skytrax (2021) *Changi Airport is voted the World's Best Airport for 8th consecutive year at the 2020 World Airport Awards* [online] https://www.worldairportawards.com/

84 Texas Medical Centre (2025) *The Largest Medical Complex in the World* [online] https://www.tmc.edu/operations/tmc-campus/

12. LIES, DAMN LIES AND...

85 NHS England (2017) *UK system comes out top in new report* [online] https://www.england.nhs.uk/2017/07/uk-health-system-comes-out-on-top-in-new-report/

86 El-Gingihy, Y. (2019) *How to dismantle the NHS in 10 easy steps* (Zero books)

87 World Population Review (2023) *Infant Mortality Rate by Country* [online] https://worldpopulationreview.com/country-rankings/infant-mortality-rate-by-country

88 World Atlas (2014) *Measles (MMR) vaccination rate by country* [online] https://www.worldatlas.com/articles/countries-with-the-highest-measles-vaccination-rates.html

89 World Health Organisation (2022) *Polio (pol3) immunization coverage among 1-year olds* [online] https://www.who.int/data/gho/data/indicators/indicator-details/GHO/polio-(pol3)-immunization-coverage-among-1-year-olds-(-)

90 Statista (2019) *Number of Magnetic Resonance Imaging (MRI) units in selected countries* [online] https://www.statista.com/statistics/282401/density-of-magnetic-resonance-imaging-units-by-country/

91 Royal College of Radiologists (2017) *NHS must do more to future proof its MRI capacity, say imaging experts* [online] https://www.rcr.ac.uk/news-policy/latest-updates/nhs-must-do-more-to-future-proof-its-mri-capacity-say-imaging-experts/

92 OECD data (2021) *Hospital Beds* [online] https://data.oecd.org/healtheqt/hospital-beds.htm

93 World Population Review (2023) *ICU beds per capacity by country* [online] https://worldpopulationreview.com/country-rankings/icu-beds-per-capita-by-country

94 The Global Economy (2020) *Doctors per 1,000 people, country rankings* [online] https://www.theglobaleconomy.com/rankings/doctors_per_1000_people/

95 The Global Economy (2020) *Nurses per 1,000 people, country rankings* [online] https://www.theglobaleconomy.com/rankings/nurses_per_1000_people/

96 Singapore Ministry of Health (2022) *Health Manpower* [online] https://www.moh.gov.sg/others/resources-and-statistics/health-manpower

97 BMA (2023) *NHS backlog date analysis* [online]
https://www.bma.org.uk/advice-and-support/nhs-delivery-and-workforce/pressures/nhs-backlog-data-analysis

98 OECD (2022) *Healthcare utilisation* [online] https://stats.oecd.org/Index.aspx?QueryId=49344

99 Commonwealth Fund (2021) *Mirror, Mirror 2021: Reflecting poorly* [online] https://www.commonwealthfund.org/publications/fund-reports/2024/sep/mirror-mirror-2024

100 The Lancet (2022) *Estimating excess mortality due to the COVID-19 Pandemic* [online] https://www.thelancet.com/article/S0140-6736(21)02796-3/fulltext

101 Worldometer (2023) *Life expectancy of world population* [online] https://www.worldometers.info/demographics/life-expectancy/

102 OECD iLibrary (2021) *Government at a Glance 2023: United Kingdom* [online] https://www.oecd.org/en/publications/government-at-a-glance-2023_c4200b14-en/united-

kingdom_7a8f7acf-en.html#:~:text=The%20United%20 Kingdom%20is%20above,%2C%20respectively%2C%20in%20 the%20OECD.

103 The Kings Fund (2022) *Public satisfaction with the NHS falls to a 25-year low* [online] https://www.kingsfund.org.uk/blog/2022/03/public-satisfaction-nhs-falls-25-year-low

104 The Health Foundation (2022) *How does UK Health spending compare across Europe over the past decade?* [online] https://www.health.org.uk/news-and-comment/charts-and-infographics/how-does-uk-health-spending-compare-across-europe-over-the-past-decade

105 The World Bank (2023) *Current Health Expenditure (% of GDP)* [online] https://data.worldbank.org/indicator/SH.XPD.CHEX.GD.ZS?end=2019&start=2019&view=bar

106 Office for National Statistics (2018) *Leading causes of death, UK 2001-2018* [online] https://www.ons.gov.uk/peoplepopulationandcommunity/healthandsocialcare/causesofdeath/articles/leadingcausesofdeathuk/2001to2018

107 Institute for Health Metrics and Evaluation (2021) *GBD Results* [online] http://ghdx.healthdata.org/gbd-results-tool

108 World Population Review (2023) *Cancer Survival Rates by Country, 2023* [online] https://worldpopulationreview.com/country-rankings/cancer-survival-rates-by-country

13. BACK IN THE USSR

109 CCTA (2021) *ONS: Average UK household income – financial year 2020* [online] https://www.ccta.co.uk/ons-average-uk-household-income-financial-year-2020/Office of Budget

110 Office for Budget Responsibility (2025) *A brief guide to the*

public finances [online] https://obr.uk/forecasts-in-depth/brief-guides-and-explainers/public-finances/

CONCLUSION

111 NHS confederation website (2022) *Drop in public satisfaction with the NHS signals need for realism about what it can deliver* [online] https://www.nhsconfed.org/news/drop-public-satisfaction-nhs-signals-need-realism-about-what-it-can-deliver

112 BBC (2023) *Ambulances taking 90 minutes to get to 999 calls* [online] https://www.bbc.co.uk/news/health-64254249

113 The Telegraph (2022) *Labour would make free access to the NHS a constitutional right* [online] https://www.telegraph.co.uk/politics/2022/12/05/labour-would-make-free-access-nhs-constitutional-right-report/#Free%20at%20Point%20of%20Need

114 Pulse Today (2023) *Labour to 'tear up' GP contract and consider move to fully salaried service* [online] https://www.pulsetoday.co.uk/news/politics/labour-to-tear-up-gp-contract-and-consider-move-to-fully-salaried-service/

www.ingramcontent.com/pod-product-compliance
Lightning Source LLC
Chambersburg PA
CBHW020520080526
44583CB00013B/676